Under The Pale
Yellow Street Lamp

Florence Diana Hunt

Dedication

This book is dedicated to my grandmother. Lillian Guinan. She told me to write a book. She knew books were in me. Took me a long time to realize she was right. They are.

Thanks...

Thanks to my husband, who said writing could be my full time job.

Thanks to my youngest son Lenny, who convinced me to get my first MacBook to write because "all authors use it." He actually found one for me that I could afford. And I like it!

Thanks to my son Bryan, who always inspired my creativity because his creativity knows no bounds.

Thanks to my sister Debbie, whose solid pursuit of her dream gave me the courage to pursue mine.

Contents

Introduction

I've always been creative. Art history came easier to me than world history. Taking maths notes looked more like drawings and poetry than equations and theorems. But I managed a couple of doctorates and a few certifications. I taught at a university in the states and in London. Then I changed careers after retiring from university life and worked in mental health as a mobile crisis peer support specialist.

One day I had a talk with my husband. You know, that talk. I said I wanted to write full-time, well, maybe part-time. He said you'll never stay sane in the house long enough to write without a way to interact with people. He was correct. I asked him how about a part-time job and part time writing? He agreed … with a catch. No teaching. No mental health. He said that both jobs consumed me. After ranting, me of course, and a few shouts of 'what do you mean?' I acquiesced, sort of. I had to tell him mental health work was in my blood, so a part-time crisis peer job it was. However, I woke up one morning soon after obtaining that part time job and knew I had to write full time, so I quit, and now I do indeed write full time. That's how I came to write this book. The first in a trilogy. With many more books to follow. And a cookbook tied to my Holmes and Flora trilogy. So let's get on with it…

Sherlock Holmes...

Since Arthur Conan Doyle's original Sherlock Holmes, writers, actors, movies, plays, radio, and TV shows have relentlessly kept Holmes and Watson alive and constantly changing. The characters have had their time separately, but they were better together. Even when given wives and families, they still end up together until very nearly the end. Watson with his practice, Holmes with his bees. This is my interpretation. Of course, not to break with something that works, you already know how this trilogy ends. Join me though. Getting there is half the fun.

Trigger warning ⚠

This book may be triggering for some. It details an attempt at sex trafficking women. While there are no complete sex scenes per se, rape and rough and brutal sex acts are alluded to and described in a way that may trigger some. This trilogy is about tough topics; sex trafficking of vulnerable women, drugs, child kidnapping and selling, and political secrets. It's grittier than some Sherlock Holmes stories. Even Sherlock isn't immune from these topics touching him personally.

The Keeper of the Flame

The pale yellow street lamp. They flocked to it like moths to a flame. Yes, moths. No butterflies were these. The butterflies were in Chelsea and Mayfair and Victoria. But here, in Whitechapel, here under the pale yellow light of the street lamp, there were only moths. Dull. Drab. Moths.

The light, a street lamp with a pale yellow flickering flame dancing along the dirty glass, cast hardly any illumination, but it was enough. The moths beneath it primped and chatted with the other moths. Can you hear them now, the moths flapping their dusky wings? Yes, they had names. Haven't we all? But not to me. The Keeper of the Flame.

I stood in the darkness between a shop door and a narrow alley and watched the moths fluttering. My moths! I watch them every night. This is where they all start, under the pale yellow street lamp. Eventually, they will fan out and go their set ways to sell their wares. The only wares they had...their bodies. I follow them. I've followed them for months. I know where they go for knee tremblers, the rare alleys that have a spot to do a lie down belly knocker, the pubs they go to spend the pennies they have earned and where they dossed for the night if all their pennies weren't spent.

Creatures of habit these moths. You'd think the moths would have learned after Jack, but no. Whitechapel had more whores than before Jack ripped the few he did. But now I'm here. Not an amateur like Jack. I have planned. I have studied. I have researched. I know what I must do. With the moths gone, the butterflies would shine. Oh, what lovely plans I have for the butterflies too.

Chapter 1

Strange Place For A Knife

"Watson, you really must stop. I'm too long a confirmed bachelor to eye a woman in any way other than to see whether she's committed the crime or not. You, my dear fellow, are the expert in everything I need to know about a woman other than that ... and only if I ask." I followed Sherlock Holmes up the 17 steps to the warmth and comfort of our rooms at 221b Baker Street.

Once in our rooms, we doffed our coats and hats on the hooks by the door and began preparations to settle in for the night. Holmes stoked the fire Mrs. Hudson had graciously set and I poured two bourbons topped with the fizzy water from the gasogene. I handed one to Holmes as I pulled my chair a bit closer to the warmth of the fire and sat. Then I looked at Holmes. "Old man, I saw her looking at you. More importantly, I also saw how you looked at her. She's a female detective and quite successful.

She thinks like you, she is like you, but I won't go there now. You listened intently to her lecture about the famous case she had just solved. Yes, not one you would have taken on, I know, but blast it, Holmes she used all your methods and solved it. By the way, exactly how did you know about this lecture in that little Whitechapel bookshop anyway? And how well do you know this woman?" With that, I took a drink. A long one. Holmes could be

3

exasperating, and he was definitely that now.

"Watson, my dear man. I admit she intrigues me. You know, she's read every tract and monograph I've written as well as your little stories." My eyes turned to saucers at that but I bit my tongue and said nothing and Holmes continued. "This woman has potential. I admit it. She works hard and gets dirty. The irregulars have seen her in action. She fights well. She's intelligent. She has promise. But that's where my interest stops, Watson. I cannot get involved. And it is my job to know about the things that go on in London, all things."

I looked at Holmes and shook my head. "Holmes, I know you pined for Miss Adler, don't deny it. But she would never have made you happy in the long run. Too fond of her conquests if you ask me. You'd be one of many and you aren't too fond of that." Holmes was preparing for a retort, but that was not meant to be.

Suddenly the door to Baker Street slammed open and a cacophony of sounds could be heard. Mrs. Hudson was screaming like a banshee over the hubbub. Holmes and I jumped out of our chairs and looked down the steps. We saw Billy at the lead with several irregulars behind him and Mrs. Hudson, still screaming, taking up the rear.

Billy, the houseboy and one of Holmes' irregulars, was struggling with a large navy and pink sack in his arms. No. Not a sack, but something sack-like. He gently laid it down on the sofa and pulled some of the material from it. It was her! The female detective that we had just heard speak a few hours ago. Flora James! Her face was quite pale, with the beginning of a nice size bruise on her cheek. She had a jeweled knife protruding from her side. She had been badly beaten in fighting off her assailant.

Her hands and arms had defensive and offensive bruising and bleeding. She had fought her assailant, and I thought she fought valiantly. I ran for my medical bag upstairs and Mrs. Hudson went to get hot water and clean cloths. Holmes knelt beside her shaking. I could tell he was taken aback. I observed him gently brushing the dark hair from her pale face as I ran.

Turning to Billy, Holmes asked him what had happened. Billy told him he had asked her to let the irregulars see her home after her lecture. She had gotten a death threat right before the speaking engagement. But she said no, that she would not cower in fear for every death threat she gets. Sherlock looked at her with pride in his eyes. Yes, she was like him.

The irregulars are street urchins Holmes sometimes used to assist him in cases. The premise is that children like that blend in and go unobserved. Therefore, they can get information easier than adults can. Sometimes they were just the eyes and ears on the street that Holmes needed. Sometimes the irregulars help those they know. This was one of those times.

Billy, out with his friends, had heard Miss James scream from three blocks away. "By the time we all gots there, Miss Flora was lying in a pool of blood. So still she was that we knowed she has to be dead. But she opened her eyes and said 'Sherlock' so we brought her here. I hope that was right." Sherlock said it was indeed the correct action and he and Billy and the other irregulars got out of the way of Doctor Watson and Mrs. Hudson.

Chapter 2

The Lovely Visitor

I stepped out of Holmes' bedroom and sat in my chair. The heat from the fire, now too hot, added to my profuse sweating. I was exhausted and put my head between my hands and sighed deeply. I laid back in the chair, letting out another louder sigh which caused a dozing Holmes to immediately jump out of his chair. "Watson! What's wrong? How's Flora?

I looked up and stared into those grey hooded eyes and shook my head to reprimand Holmes. "She needs a hospital, Holmes, not your chambers on Baker Street. She's lost a lot of blood. I stitched her. Without morphine, I might add." Holmes winced at this remark. "Flora is as stubborn as you. She refused a hospital by citing your monograph on bacterial infections caught in hospital settings resulting in patients' deaths! She's resting now with orders not to so much as sit up lest her stitches tear." Mrs. Hudson will stay with her, and I will check on her every few hours. Holmes seemed content with this and returned to his chair, pulling tighter around him the mouse-colored dressing gown he was wearing. Billy lay sleeping on the sofa, wrapped lightly in a blanket and in the arms of Morpheus, God of Sleep, which we will certainly not be tonight. The other irregulars left to return from whence they came. Holmes and I turned when we heard the bedroom door crack open. Mrs. Hudson poked her head out and whispered, "Sherlock, she wants to see you."

I looked at Holmes and said, "please, keep this short. If she doesn't rest, she could die." Holmes nodded that he understood as he swept past Mrs. Hudson and me, quietly shooing her, much to her distress, outside the bedroom and closing the door.

I stood watching Flora nodding in and out of sleep, tossing in restless pain. The lamp by the bed was lit low, and Flora's black hair, loose and in wavy curls, was laid out on my pillow. Her hair seemed to glow with the flame of the lamp. My sharp intake of breath must have awakened her from her fitful rest. She opened her eyes, looked at me, and winced in the throes of pain as another wave wracked her body. "Sherlock," she said softly. I knelt beside the bed and once again brushed her hair softly away from her face. "The problem in the West End, in Whitechapel, you know of it?"

"Yes,' I said. "Women disappearing. Flora, were you to be one of those women?" Flora closed her eyes and whispered a soft yes. "Well then, we shall discuss this in a few days when you are feeling better." I stood and looked at this amazingly brave woman, hesitated thoughtfully for a moment, and bent to gently kiss her forehead. She smiled in her sleep. I then slipped out of the room and the protective Mrs. Hudson swept back in and closed the door glaring at me as she went.

Chapter 3

Questions

A full three days later, I allowed Miss Flora James to be seated on the sofa in our flat for the first time. Holmes had not spoken about the circumstances of Flora's injuries as I had requested, but today I have allowed her to be briefly questioned. She was surrounded by pillows. Every pillow Mrs. Hudson owned I feared.

She was wrapped in Holmes' mouse-coloured dressing gown with the sleeves rolled up. Her hair was pulled up and she was still quite pale. The bruise on her cheek had reached full colour and was beginning to fade around the edges. I had determined that asking a few pertinent questions would be acceptable and could help ascertain who the culprit was that could beat and stab a woman in the middle of the night.

She told us that she had turned the corner to enter the street on which she lived and was grabbed from behind. She had seen the glint of the knife and assumed she was going to be killed, a good assumption to make in Whitechapel, and she, therefore, reacted accordingly. Flora knew the streets well and knew that to stay alive, one must fight. I can assume she was as good a fighter as the irregulars and Holmes had said she was because here she was in our flat. Alive and healing.

"Did he speak to you, Flora?" Holmes was gentle and calm in his questions to her. I could see he was choosing the questions and his words carefully. He was leaning forward, elbows on his knees and hands steepled under his chin, and watching her, reading her as she thought back to that night. Flora had closed her eyes and was deep in thought for the next few moments. Holmes was silent as he waited for her answer. His usual lack of patience was gone.

"Yes, he spoke to me. He called me a moth. He said, 'you are a pretty little moth. You will look good in my collection.' I knew then that if I didn't fight, I'd never be seen again, at least not alive. I know he must be the one responsible for the women in Whitechapel disappearing. I feel it. I know that's strange, but I feel strongly that he has a purpose for them by the way he said his 'collection.' Though what that purpose might be, I do not yet know."

She looked at Holmes. "I fought hard, just like I saw you do when you're fighting in the West End boxing dens." Holmes lifted an eyebrow. "Yes, I watched you. Don't act like you didn't know I was too. I saw you watching me as I made my way around the betting tables. I always bet on you, by the way."

Holmes blushed to the tips of his ears, and I looked at him with the satisfaction that I had been right in my earlier conversation with him of a few days ago. He cleared his throat, scowled at me, and continued his questions. "Flora, did you get a look at him? From your description so far, he was behind you. Yet you have defensive and offensive bruising on your arms and hands. At what point did you turn to face your attacker?"

Flora thought hard, and though she tried, she didn't seem to be able to recall when she turned. "Sherlock, it happened so fast and there's virtually no light there. Well, except for that pale yellow street lamp. It's so filthy and turned so low that unless you are right under it, it's useless.

I do remember I turned by ducking under his arm and twisting my body to follow around him after he said I was for his collection. But he hit me in the face to try and prevent me from seeing him. But I'll tell you all I do remember from that point. He smelled old. Musty old. His clothes had an odd smell, and a pungent one. His breath was horrible, like food, tobacco, and drink, a lot of it. Before I twisted around him, I looked down and saw the tip of one shoe. Shiny. Well kept. Brown.

A short boot, I think. Oxfords, not brogues. His jacket was brown as well. Wool. It scratched me. His hair was greasy, no, no, not greasy, but pomaded and dark. No beard, a slight fashionable mustache. No cap either, though I could have knocked it off when I turned. His hands were smooth and I smelled something sweet on them. A chemical sweetness, I think. Sorry, that's all. Then we were fighting. I heard footsteps running toward me. I got him down, then he stabbed me and ran. I was bleeding so badly I could smell my blood. I screamed. Then I woke up here. I ... I ... Sherlock, I'm not feeling well."

Flora turned deathly pale and collapsed back on the sofa, nearly falling off it. Holmes grabbed her gently and hooked his arms under her slight body. He carried her effortlessly back to his bed and bade me check her health. Her breathing was strong and even. She had just fainted. "Holmes, old man, she overexerted her mind telling that story, I'm afraid. She's fine but needs rest. Let's step into the other room and let her get some restorative sleep. I'll leave the door open. We will be near if she needs us."

Back in the other room, we took our seats and Holmes grabbed his Persian slipper and began to fill his pipe. I lit my cigar. He stopped before he lit the pipe and looked at me with concern in his eyes. "Watson, did I push her too hard?"

"Holmes, no, no, you didn't." I looked at him reassuringly. "I've never known you to be so considerate before in your questioning. Her injuries will take some time to heal. The mental injuries will take even longer. We are finding that trauma can badly affect the mind. That these traumas can take longer to heal than physical injuries. We are referring many patients who have experienced trauma to see psychiatrists like your friend Freud." He seemed to find relief in my words because he picked up the pipe again and continued to fill it.

Next to the pipe was the knife we found on Flora's side. It wasn't a long one, but the blade was unusually sharp, and the handle was jeweled with rubies. "Holmes, shouldn't you give that knife to Lestrade as evidence?" I asked. Holmes looked at the knife, picked it up, then placed it in the side table drawer under his pipe rack. "I think not, Watson. I feel we will find this knife more important than we think and I'd like it close by if that's the case."

He sat for a moment longer and then he jumped up from his chair and began pacing the room. A beaming smile was across his face. "Watson, did you listen to her details? All she saw, smelled, heard, and observed. Even under duress, she was brilliant like me. He stopped and looked at me with one brow raised and looking down that aquiline nose of his. Yes, Watson, don't look so surprised. You are correct. She is a lot like me. Oh, were it only so that all my clients, the police, and even you were as observant. She is a gem, my Flora." I looked at Holmes. His eyes were sparkling. He was smiling. A rare thing indeed from him.

Oh, but this was too good to let go by. "Holmes? 'Your Flora?' That's a nice turn of words. I think I'm also correct in our conversation a few days ago about your feelings for her." I picked up my cigar and relit it.

Then Holmes said something that would have made me drop to the ground had I not been sitting. As it was, I dropped my cigar and quickly picked it up and patted out the sparks before they could catch. He said that yes, I was right about that part of our conversation too!

Holmes did not give me a second to gloat before he became quite serious and said, "we have something evil going on in Whitechapel again and they will not make me sit this one out and silence me as they did with the other one." I knew that the Ripper case was still a sore subject for Holmes. Then he put down his pipe, bade me goodnight, and of all things, he entered his bedroom where Flora was sleeping and closed the door!

Chapter 4

Tables Turned

When I came down from my room, drawn by the lovely scent of Mrs. Hudson's delicious breakfast food, I came upon a surreal sight. Holmes and Flora were up and having tea and some of Mrs. Hudson's excellent breakfast scones with jam and clotted cream. Mrs. Hudson was playing mother, pouring tea and doling out scones and clotted cream and strawberry jam, and the scene looked uncanny. It was even more so when Billy, who was standing by the door, was told by Holmes to let Inspector Lestrade enter and Holmes invited him to breakfast with us. I hadn't even heard Lestrade come up the steps. Holmes, however, had a preternatural hearing.

"Watson, there you are, old man, Flora and I almost gave up hope of seeing you today!" My mouth was still hanging open when Holmes turned to Flora and softly kissed her cheek, added jam and cream to her scone, and passed it to her." Flora beamed at him.

The scent of the Earl Grey, along with freshly made scones, prevented me from commenting further. I found my place and accepted a cup of the fragrant brew from Mrs. Hudson. I then took two lovely and warm scones and put them on my plate along with lashings of sweet strawberry jam and smooth and buttery clotted cream. Heaven!

There was no talk of what happened to Flora nor the

disappearance of Whitechapel's women until after Mrs. Hudson and Billy had cleared the remnants of our meal and retreated downstairs. Holmes reported to Lestrade about Flora's attack, with her adding bits and pieces as her memory was triggered by the conversation. She was beginning to remember more now.

Lestrade then told us what he knew about the disappearances of the women, which was not much more than names, sometimes only the first name, and where they were last reported being seen before they went missing. "Sherlock," he said, "we have reports that they were missing from the landlords of their doss houses because they owed back rent and sometimes from pimps who, again, were owed money. This was only because money was owed, or we might never have known they were missing at all. No one reports missing, unfortunates unless there is something in it for them or they are owed something."

"And names," Lestrade said, "that's even worse. We have a 'Jane something' or 'I think her name rhymed with cat.' Add to that the fact that most of the unfortunates make up names to stay hidden from people or to protect the few family members they still have. You know that *these women* are hard to track and impossible to find."

With that, Flora turned to Lestrade, eyes blazing, and calmly placed her cup and saucer on the table in front of her and looked him in the eye. "*These women*! *These women*! Inspector, do you mean to say that *these women* are worth less than the women of Chelsea, or Victoria, or Mayfair? I was one of *these women* not too long ago. So do you mean I am less than too?"

Lestrade sputtered and choked trying to form words, the right words, to get his foot, or should I say feet, out of his mouth. Holmes was sitting back on the sofa, smiling. I waited too, with rapt attention, for Lestrade to speak. "Miss James, first, I'm sorry about how my words sounded. Second, I meant no disrespect. But you must know that leaving a trail, witnesses, family, or someone willing to speak to us rarely happens in Whitechapel's streets. Even when women were being ripped a few years back no one would help us. So, though we try, we are left with nowhere to go."

Lestrade was genuinely sorry, and Flora eased his mind. "Please," she said, "let me explain. The women you called *these women* helped me after a bad time in my life. I was still a newly recovering opium addict. I had little money. I lost my lodgings suddenly. When I told these kind women I wanted to be a private detective, they could have laughed, but they didn't. They took up a collection all over Whitechapel. A fund me on the go, you could say." Flora took a sip of her tea.

Then she continued her story. "They collected enough for me to do a…. a…. a private detective start-up. They also talked to the local butcher, who had recently lost his greengrocer from the storefront room he had been renting, into giving me that room rent free for a year by saying my business would bring customers in for him! They believed in me. I started again in life, which is very rare indeed in Whitechapel, so forgive me if I want respect for them."

"Inspector, I also know what you say is true. I remember the lack of communication the police suffered during the time of Jack the Ripper. Please don't give up though. They deserve more than to be forgotten once they are gone. Most of them have no one anymore. Besides, I have a feeling they aren't dead. At least not yet. My attacker referred to his collection. Did Sherlock tell you?"

Lestrade cut in, "yes, I know. Moths or butterflies or something."

Flora suddenly grabbed Holmes by the arm. "Sherlock, I remember something else. He said butterflies. He said when the moths are done, he will collect butterflies." We looked from her to Holmes.

"Butterflies," Holmes stated. "Well, we have more of a problem than we thought. If the women of Whitechapel are seen as moths, then the butterflies must be in the more well-to-do areas of London. No woman in London is safe."

Chapter 5

Another Gone

With Holmes' last frightening statement hanging in the air there was a desperate pounding on the downstairs door. Then we heard the sound of police issued boots swiftly running up the stairs. Our door flew open, and Inspector Gregson stood there breathless for a moment. We all stared at him as he leaned forward, hands on knees and swayed to steady himself. I rushed to him and bade him to sit down and gave him a restorative brandy.

Pale and still winded, he spoke. "There's been another abduction," he exclaimed. "Last night. A Miss Rose Taylor. The woman who shared a room across the street with her said that was her name anyway. Said she recognised her voice when she was screaming for help. As you know, help rarely comes in Whitechapel and it didn't come for Rose. She was abducted near where Miss James lives by that pale yellow street lamp. The narrow alley. Across the street. Blood everywhere. Oh, God." I presented him with another medicinal brandy.

Flora's hand went to her throat and she visibly paled. "Rose is my best friend. Oh no. I can't believe this. Sherlock, we must go to the scene. We must speak to her roommate immediately. We need details to solve this, and we won't get them sitting here."

Holmes held Flora gently on each shoulder, so she faced toward him. He looked into her eyes and said, "Flora, I'm going right now but you cannot. It's too soon. You have many internal stitches that need to heal. Watson here would never forgive me if I let you go. I promise I'll come back and tell you everything. Billy and Mrs. Hudson will stay with you. I promise we will be solving this case together, but you need to rest a few more days. Flora, give me your word you'll stay here."

Reluctantly, Flora agreed and sank back in her seat among the pillows on the sofa. "Sherlock, promise to come back as soon as you can," she said softly to him. He nodded his head and turned.

"Come, Watson. Lestrade, I assume your officers know by now to leave my crime scenes untouched. Gregson, lead on. The game is afoot." Holmes had his coat in hand as he headed for the stairs with the rest of us trailing him.

I turned to Flora. "If you keep healing as well as you've been, in a few days I will consider letting you actively back into the investigation." I hesitated briefly, then said, "Flora, you are good for him. I hope he is good for you too." I left with Flora smiling on the sofa. A pretty picture to hold in my mind until I arrived at that bloody alley.

Chapter 6

Holmes' Find

The constables had marked off the scene at Gregson's orders because they knew Sherlock Holmes would be on the way. As we arrived, we congregated near the officer in charge while Gregson and Lestrade spoke with him. Holmes, however, turned and went straight to the scene itself, the dark, dank, bloody alley. We watched as he did his first walkthrough, just noticing things immediately apparent to him. Then he began his examination in earnest.

He took his magnifying glass from his pocket and was on the ground every few feet, examining every cobblestone. Calling for more light. Grabbing lanterns at arm's length lest the scene be disturbed. At one point, he took a tweezer from his pocket and a glassine envelope as well. He bent with his nose almost down to the filthy ground and gently lifted something with the tweezer and placed it in the envelope. Once the envelope was in his pocket, Holmes resumed his examination. This time he sniffed at the wall in a few places around where the most blood had been spattered. He shook his head and smiled. Then he paced the scene and the street in front of it, making several sweeps of each. Noticing things, disregarding things, committing things to his mind palace, the place in his brain where he stores his facts and necessary information and deletes the rest like a machine.

Lestrade, Gregson, and I watched Holmes finish his pacing with one last sweep of the alley and walk back to us. "Holmes, were there any clues?" I asked. The three of us were waiting for Holmes to tell us something, anything more than the little bits of tiny facts we already knew. We needed to stop these disappearances and find these women. Facts were the exact things we were keenly aware were in short supply.

Holmes took a long breath and sighed. "I can tell you that Rose put up a valiant fight. A fight almost as good as Flora did when she fought off her abductor, I believe the same abductor. The patterns of the blood indicate a moving struggle. I think he was lashing out with a knife, probably cutting her arms in the process and holding her with the other hand to try to stop her from getting away like Flora did. He finally succeeded in regaining purchase with her near the end of the alley by the street. Notice the blood stopped there. A hansom picked them up. It could not have been waiting too far away. We are not dealing with one person. He is borrowing from our Jack, but he is much smarter than Jack was, and he learned from Jack's mistakes. He's done his homework and I'm afraid if we don't do ours he, rather they, might get away."

Watson looked to the end of the alley and said, "Holmes, I noticed you picked something up and you also smiled when you smelled something along the walls, I believe." All three men waited for the explanation of Watson's statement.

"Ah," said Holmes, "Watson, you are observing and seeing more. Good man."

"Yes, I smelled Flora's 'musty old' smell. Apparently, he was thrown into the wall in a few places. The smell was easily transferred by rubbing his coat against the damp walls. Mothballs Watson! It was mothballs! That was the old smell Flora told us she remembered. Interesting that. I also smelled slight traces of chloroform, the sweet chemical smell Flora described. It will be a three-pipe problem tonight, I think. Gentlemen, that's all I can tell you for now."

"But Holmes," I sputtered, "what of the item you retrieved. The item in the glassine envelope in your jacket pocket?" But Holmes had already turned and was hailing a hansom to return us to Baker Street.

"Watson, it's too early to discuss that. I must think. I must sort facts. Come, leave Lestrade and Gregson to their work here and their interview of Rose's roommate. I doubt she knows more. Probably heard the screams, of which there definitely were some, and reported it because she would be out of money at the end of the week to pay rent. Let us return and tell Flora what we have learned."

Chapter 7

What Envelope?

Leaving the police to canvas the streets and query the roommate, we rode in silence back to Baker Street, where Holmes told Flora of our outing. He confirmed the smell of mothballs and that it was an important clue. It was what Flora had smelled when she was attacked. He also confirmed the sweet smell that Flora smelled, it was chloroform. Holmes assured her that the inspectors would question Rose's roommate but not to expect new information from that. Then, he dug in his vest pocket for the glassine envelope.

"Watson has been very curious as to what I found in the cobbles, and I'm sure you will be too, Flora." He then tipped the contents of the envelope out in his hand. In his palm was a tiny straight pin. It was clean except for a small drop of congealed blood at the non-pointy end. Flora and I looked at Holmes quizzically.

"A pin Holmes?" I asked. "It's just a pin. A plain straight pin."

"No, Watson, it is an entomological pin. A pin used by lepidopterists to secure their specimens of moths and butterflies. It does not rust like straight sewing pins would. It seems these men, because we now know there is more than one, have been collecting the insects, moths and butterflies, before they became collectors of women. This gives us a starting place for our inquiries. It is also a pastime of the more well to do. The upper classes. We can now begin to understand who our collector is and question proprietors of lepidopterist shops and lepidoptery clubs. There can't be more than one or two of these shops or clubs in London. I will need to think about this and develop questions and a plan."

Holmes placed the pin back in the glassine envelope and placed it back in his pocket.

Then Holmes continued. "When we add to this Flora's statement about smelling something musty and old, and the mothball scent that I smelled at the latest abduction scene, and that Flora most definitely smelled at her attempted abduction, we have the beginning of a theory. Think about this: the seasons have just recently changed, have they not?"

"Yes. So, clothes for cooler weather, stored over summer, are now coming out. I would vouch that not one of Whitechapel's poor has clothes for every season. Definitely not clothes carefully packed away and stored with mothballs. Add lepidoptery, a hobby of the idle rich, and you can deduce these are people with money." Holmes moved to the window and looked out.

"Holmes, are you saying it's someone of the upper class abducting these poor women?" I asked.

"Watson, I am not saying anything without more facts. I do not guess or speculate. I am merely stating we have a direction to follow."

Holmes went to the table beside his chair and filled his first pipe of the three he usually needed to think through a problem.

Flora, quiet all this time, stood and stretched. She walked to the fireplace and with the tongs she grabbed an ember to light Holmes' pipe. He sat in his chair and stared into the flames, already oblivious to even Flora. The smoke began to rise around his head, and he was in his mind palace trying to put some of these clues together to find a direction for the case investigation to head.

It was only late afternoon, and I knew Holmes was not going to be hungry or stop for food. Flora needed to eat as she was still early in the healing process. And we all know I am not one to miss a meal. I prefer them regularly and often if you please. Our Mrs. Hudson would be out with Billy at her church's volunteer site for a few more hours and I had already missed lunch. I turned to Flora and said, "Holmes will not know we exist for hours. If you will permit me, as your physician and your friend, to escort you to a late lunch at Simpson's, I can promise I won't bore you with my war stories."

Flora looked at me and smiled. "My dear doctor Watson, I would be honoured to have you as my dinner companion and very happy to get out of the house as well." She slipped into Holmes' room to ready herself and I discreetly went to the table by my chair and slipped the Webley from the drawer into my coat pocket. After all, 'he,' 'they', were still out there and, for all we know, still after Flora. No chances would be taken in protecting her.

The Keeper of the Flame

No! She won't escape me again. She fought like a fiend. But I saw the potential for her to realize who I am. That would not do at all. I let her go with a non-fatal stab. I even lost my favourite knife in her after I heard footfalls and had to run. It was my uncle Jack's knife. A gift to me with a similar one gifted to my best friend. I shall have it back, I assure you. But next time, this moth will be mine. My moth who thinks she's a butterfly. I'll teach her place again. Just like last time.

She was always acting above her station. Convincing my poor sister she was her friend, and then begging my father to allow her to take lessons alongside her was despicable. My father didn't know how to treat women. Always giving them what they wanted, but not what they needed. But she refused my advances even then. Fought me. A bloody servant girl. But she was taught her place.

After my return from university and another advance rebuffed, plans were made. My friends, who were also spurned by her, and I made plans. Why couldn't she just let us have her like any low-class servant girl would have done? She should have welcomed the chance to bed with one of us, let alone all of us. But she thought she was too good for us. She learned the error of her ways.

We drugged her one night. Her coffee. She liked to have a cup whilst she studied her lessons. Lessons paid for by my pathetic father and encouraged by my stupid sister. Then we administered opium. I had her first. Then all my friends had her. Over and over and in every orifice, till the morning, we took our turns. Brutally.

We drugged her again and bound and gagged her, naked as a moth should be, and put her in a long-abandoned room in my father's home. My parents assumed she had run away. My sister cried for a while. But my friends and I drugged her and took her over and over for weeks. Day and night. When we were thoroughly bored with her, I drugged her and bound her and sold her to the lowest brothel in London I could find. She was now addicted to the generous amount of opium we supplied and would lie with anyone or anything to get it. Then I forgot about the bitch.

Suddenly, one day whilst in London, I saw her! She was healthy and in clothes that were still moth drab but fashionable. What I saw next was even more shocking. She was a detective. A private detective with her own storefront. It was then I knew I was born to teach these moths a lesson to show them all they are good for was a man's pleasure. Butterflies, too, thanks to my sister. But that's another story.

Chapter 8

Flora and Watson

Simpsons looked as lovely as ever. Impeccable staff, beautifully laid tables, shining chandeliers, and the intoxicating smell of good food and drink well prepared. Flora and I were seated well away from the windows for privacy. Flora still looked pale but was up to the outing, in my medical opinion. My first question to her was, "How long were you addicted to opium?"

She took a calming breath and told me her story. I heard about her early life and the abuse that she suffered under the hands of madmen. She told me about the bordello where she lived after being sold and how she met a woman, another unfortunate, Rose, who helped her with her addiction and with getting free of the bordello. When she had finished, she took a sip of tea, her hand shaking the teacup, and waited quietly for my response.

"Oh, Flora. I'm so terribly sorry for all you had to endure at their hands and because of them. Does Holmes know?" Flora shook her head yes.

"Your addiction is well controlled then. It's why you didn't want morphine, isn't it?" She whispered, "yes."

"He hasn't bothered you since then, has he, this…. this…. this devil?"

Flora put her hand over mine and leaned close.

"No, Doctor Watson. I haven't seen or heard from him. It's a chapter of my life long over and though I endured much, I learned much. I suspect Sherlock and I have a lot in common that way, learning from past trauma. It's why we are sometimes moody, sometimes blue, and sometimes we can work without sleep or sustenance. It is also why we fell in love with each other as quickly as we did. We are soulmates. We see each other's wounded souls and we love each other in spite of the pain we see." She pushed back in her seat and her eyes misted in thought.

I gave her the time she needed to compose herself. I thought about these two brilliant people drawn together by their wounds. They had both suffered their traumas silently until now. There was a bond, a beautiful bond that had bloomed immediately when they met. And now comes the test, a test of their minds in trying to find these women. If anyone can figure this out, it will be these two.

We had been gone a few hours enjoying our meal and getting to know each other. Flora had a lovely soup, Chicken De La Reine, the Queen's soup, as she was still healing, and I recommended a light meal. I had a wonderful roast with potatoes and carrots. The conversation was also light and delightful. Time flew by. I knew I should return to Baker Street soon or Holmes would worry.

"Flora, shall we head back home?" She woke from her thoughts and asked if we could stop at her flat. She needed some things. I agreed and pulled her chair out for her to rise.

We headed to the door and suddenly Flora grabbed my arm. "Doctor Watson!" She exclaimed. I thought there was a medical problem and grabbed her shoulders lest she falls to the ground in a faint but she pushed my hands away.

"Do you smell it? Mothballs!"

She was right. There was a distinct aroma, though faint, of mothballs. The restaurant was now very crowded, and though we looked around us, ...shall we say.... we lost the scent. We left and the doorman fetched us a hansom. We went to Flora's flat, where she brought out four suitcases and various bags. A few things, indeed! Flora then told me that her address would now be 221b Baker Street. She apologized that she hadn't mentioned it earlier. Holmes had asked her to move in shortly before Scotland Yard came to fetch him to the crime scene where her friend Rose was abducted. I said I was quite glad for there to be a trio in our humble home, and she leaned over and kissed my cheek. I knew I was blushing because my collar became quite tight! We then headed home to Baker Street.

Chapter 9

Someone of Means

As soon as we arrived back at Baker Street, Billy and I brought Flora's things into Holmes' room while she told him about the smell of mothballs at Simpson's and how we had just lost the scent. Holmes had that glint in his eyes when a budding theory of his proved true. He waited until Billy returned downstairs and came and sat with us.

"It is as I believed. We are looking for someone of means. Someone who has either no family or family that cannot or will not see the fiend in their midst. Maybe they do and that's his accomplice. The family does not include a wife, for a wife would instruct staff on how to remove the unpleasant mothballs scent from the clothes before wearing them. However, this person has a place where these women are being held. Flora may be right; these women might be alive for a reason. But they may not be held where they are now for long if I'm correct. We need to plan."

I immediately said, "Holmes, you do not believe these women are dead?" He shook his head no, "Watson, you know London gives up her dead easily. There have been no reports of bodies or of body parts, no floaters in the Thames, nothing in the last few weeks except for a few males whose deaths were wholly explainable by Scotland Yard. We aren't looking for dead men.

While I was at Scotland Yard today checking with Lestrade and Gregson to see if any other bodies had been found, I asked them to join us for coffee. Mrs. Hudson has outdone herself with one of her Victoria Sponge cakes and as I did not choose to eat at all today, I must appease her by having dessert. I thought we could pool our knowledge since we last met as we enjoy our coffee."

With that, Mrs. Hudson swept into the room with a tray to place her cake on our table, along with coffee, cream, and sugar. It looked magnificent. It was made to honour Queen Victoria, a lover of sweets and afternoon tea, just like me. Billy was downstairs answering the door and telling our guests to go up the stairs and join us. After they entered, Mrs. Hudson exited, taking young Billy, who had climbed the stairs in hopes of having cake, and closed the door behind her. Both inspectors greeted Flora, then Holmes and me. We bade them sit and Holmes poured the coffee as Flora cut the cake. Lestrade and Gregson were made comfortable, and we ate as we talked.

Lestrade spoke first. "We canvassed the area by the abduction of Miss Taylor. No one we could find saw or heard a thing. Impossible if you ask me, but that's all we've got. The roommate knew nothing besides what she said at her report, she heard screaming and crying for help and could tell it was Rose who was being attacked. Gregson can explain his assignment and what he found." He turned to Gregson and bade him speak.

Gregson swallowed a piece of cake he was chewing and began. "I was asked to find the homeless who use the area to bed down for the night. They are sometimes good sources of information for us. Usually, they choose recessed doorways to businesses closed for the evening to help them stay out of the wind and the elements. Some have regular spots, but some are travellers. They go from area to area. We spoke to several of the homeless we found. On that night, they heard or saw nothing. One regular who uses the doorway closest to the alley that could have helped us was late getting to his spot that night." He stopped to sip his coffee and take a bite of cake.

Gregson then continued, "However, several of the homeless said there has been a man who stands in the shadow of that alley. He has been there many times in the last several months. He watches the unfortunates who gather under the pale yellow street lamp as they primp before they leave for the night's work. I couldn't get a solid description. Most of these homeless are drunk as they bed down for the night. But they did say he was well dressed for that area and after the ladies left, a coach came for him."

Holmes thought for a second, then said, "Gregson, where can a coach wait and not be observed by the ladies but can see them leave or see a signal from our abductor to pick him up?"

Gregson didn't hesitate, "there's no place that a coach could stop where the ladies wouldn't see it. The street by the lamp the ladies use can be observed from that alley if parked far enough up the curve of the road. But anyone driving the coach would need a signal because they would not be able to see a hand wave, or a hat being shaken or the like. That area is way too dark for that."

"Lestrade," Holmes said as he jumped up from his chair, "I need to go back to that alley immediately. I have a theory and I need to see if I'm correct. If I am, I have definitely missed something during my first look at the alley. Gregson, while I'm gone, can you and Flora see if you can figure out the days the homeless you spoke with saw the man. Flora, see if you can also remember ever seeing the coach, the man, or someone watching the ladies under the lamp. Watson, come with me." As he was putting on his coat, he added, "Oh, and list the days the women' disappeared too." He called to Lestrade, who was eating his last mouthful of cake, to hurry as he bounded down the stairs.

Flora asked Mrs. Hudson for more coffee. Gregson and Flora began to draw out sightings and match days to Gregson's notes. Both were working studiously to draw up an easily readable timeline on Sherlock's chalkboards.

Chapter 10

Holmes Makes a Mistake

Holmes began under the pale yellow street lamp. The watery yellow tinged light barely illuminated him. He looked down the streets, from that viewpoint, in every direction. Lestrade and I stood outside of the entrance to the narrow alley across from the street lamp and observed Holmes at work. He paced down one street, first one way, then the other. He walked up the street where the pale yellow street lamp was and we saw him enter the curve in the street where the ladies wouldn't be able to see the coach but the driver would be able to see someone in the alley if a signal were given. Gregson was correct. There would need to be a signal. We could barely see Holmes. We definitely could not see if he raised a hand or waved. Then he walked quickly back to us, swooped by us, then right past us!

"Holmes! I yelled." But he just entered the mouth of the alley and looked down. He backed up till just past the filthy gutter. Then he stood stock still looking down. We joined him and we saw. There on the litter strewn street were spent matches. Now that we saw them, it seemed they were everywhere. That was the signal, a flaming matchstick.

"Oh, Watson," said Holmes with a downcast look. I did indeed miss the meaning of this the first time we were here. "This error was inexcusable." We entered Lestrade's police coach and headed back to Baker Street.

Arriving back at 221b, we entered to see Mrs. Hudson pouring coffee and Gregson and Flora frantically transcribing notes onto two of Holmes' chalkboards. Flora turned too quickly at the sound of Holmes' voice, and she clutched at her side and began stumbling. Seeping between her fingers was blood. I saw all colour drain from Holmes' face as he ran to her. She wrapped her arms around him, and he swept her up and carried her to the bedroom bellowing for me to grab my bag and come as he did so.

Everyone else was frozen in place. Mrs. Hudson ran to the bedroom before I could do as Holmes asked and grab my bag and get there. Gregson and Lestrade just stood and stared at Holmes as he carried Flora into the bedroom. When we had all entered the bedroom and the door closed, they sat and waited to see what had happened.

In the bedroom, I saw immediately that Flora was fine, Holmes, however, was not. Flora had just pulled a few stitches with the sudden turn and all the commotion of the day. I had mentioned to them earlier that she was lucky the knife was a short one and not a long dagger. She was healing well. I applied a pressure bandage, and she was fine, but I thought I would need smelling salts for Holmes. His cheeks were beginning to get some colour after Flora sat up and then stood with his assistance. Flora wanted to get back to things. Holmes said she should rest. Flora won, of course, and led Holmes by the hand back out to the waiting inspectors.

With everyone seated but Flora and Gregson, Mrs. Hudson once again began pouring coffee and our information session resumed.

Chapter 11

Making the First Plan

Flora began first. "You see here on my board the days that I remember seeing a coach near the end of my street. Of course, it isn't the only days, I'm sure. I couldn't remember more than these, but you will see that it is enough for our purposes. You also must remember that seeing a coach, a nice one, is not abnormal in Whitechapel. Many wealthy men come there to seek companionship, gamble, and to frequent the opium dens. Most people who live there ignore these coaches. They are more interested in what and who is in them and how much money they can get from them. I don't, however, remember seeing a man there in the alley."

Gregson turned his board to us. The board showed the disappearances of the six women and the days the homeless remembered seeing a coach, a man, or the ladies. "As you can see," he began, "they remembered the coach hardly at all, the man more than that, and they remembered the women the most because seeing them corresponded with the time they began to seek the best shelter to sleep for the night. I'm sure you all can see the pattern here."

We could indeed. On the days listed on the side of Gregson's board, Flora also noticed a coach and the homeless noticed either a coach or the man.

Holmes spoke first. "We definitely have a pattern. We also can be fairly certain that there are at least two men involved. And the means is a coach. Lestrade, we need to put men in the area. They need to look local or homeless, and they need to start tonight. That the means is a coach is obvious in these abductions. Had I only understood the meaning of matches in the gutter the other night..."

Flora jumped up with startling speed. "No! You do not get to do that. You do not get to second guess yourself. Sherlock, we are much farther along with this case now and it was thanks to you, so please stop this nonsense now." Flora coyly smiled at him and winked at me when out of his line of vision. "You wouldn't want me to pull another stitch, would you?" Holmes sat immediately and Lestrade, with a brief smile, began to speak. I squeezed Flora's hand in gratitude. Holmes can easily fall into one of his blue moods when he feels he doesn't live up to his own reputation.

"We are tight with available men as the holidays are approaching, this being mid-November, but I will see what I can do. I might ask those willing to earn overtime to sign up for four hour shifts in Whitechapel in plainclothes. Just might be able to do it that way." said Lestrade.

Gregson was shaking his head yes to that plan and had already drawn up a sheet for the men to sign if they wanted to earn extra money for the holidays. "Sir," he said to Lestrade, "I will leave for Scotland Yard now if you don't mind and get this sheet in place for a shift change so the men can begin signing up."

Lestrade waved him off and Gregson bade his farewells and was on his way. Lestrade soon bade his farewells, too and was off to see his wife and tell her this would be another long haul for him. He was blessed that she understood police work. He was not sure she would be so understanding so close to the holidays. Such is the life of a police inspector.

"Well, now that our good inspectors are gone," said Holmes, "Watson, do you feel like accompanying me to the lepidopterist shop on Oxford Street? It's the only one in London." I answered in the affirmative and Holmes said, "do wear something a bit shabby...but chic."

"Ha!" I exclaimed. "That's a style for you, shabby chic. Maybe it will come into vogue someday," I laughed. I stood and went to my room to see what I had to dress as Holmes had asked.

I took Flora by the hand and led her to the bedroom. Once inside, I closed the door and bade her lie down on the bed to rest. Once her head was on the pillow, I kissed her softly. When the kiss broke, I looked at her. "Flora, I need you to rest. You have amazing strength, but you are pushing yourself much too hard. I need you to recuperate fully. I have a feeling you will be needed later in this investigation. I want you to be strong. For what I think is coming, you must be strong" I grabbed the quilt from the foot of the bed and covered her gently. Then I went to our closet to see what I had to change into for my foray with Watson.

I watched him change into the clothes he chose for his visit to the lepidoptery shop with Doctor Watson. I watched the way he moved, like a panther, slowly and gracefully. His clothes, even this costume he was now wearing, fit impeccably. He was sinewy and elegant, and I loved him beyond reason. I knew him on a deep level. I knew his mind well before I knew the man by reading his tracts and monographs. I purposely based my skill set on him. I knew he solved crimes and in Whitechapel, I had to be able to do so as well. I was passionate about that after Jack had killed some of my dearest friends. Older women who encouraged me to get off the streets. They saw my ability, skill, and education and could not understand why I was walking the streets selling my body like they did. They had no choice. After my rape and captivity led to my addiction, I thought I didn't either.

Flora stopped to think back to those days as she was falling asleep. When Flora was unfortunate, she had her one room. Her Palace. The only thing she thought was truly hers. But Jack took that from her. After what happened in that room, she could never go back. She had let that young girl, so much like a younger version of herself before she learned the way of the world, stay in her room while she walked the streets to earn money. And now that young girl was dead. It should have been her, Mary, in that room, but it was the innocent Flora. Mary stopped selling her body that day. Mary was gone and Flora James was born again like the phoenix from the flames. Exhausted, she turned and slept.

I lowered the flame in the lamp beside the bed and looked at Flora, now asleep. She had told me her story, all of it, including who she really was. I didn't think I would ever find love, but I finally had it, and it was precious to me. She is precious to me. I intend to marry her; I know that much. But later, after this case. I know Flora will think of nothing else until this madman is held accountable and her friend is found, hopefully alive. Yes, she is indeed a lot like me.

Chapter 12

The Lepidoptery Shop

The bell on the door jingled as we two gentlemen entered the shop. We began perusing the shelves seeing large collections of butterflies and moths pinned neatly on velvet, under glass, and hanging on the walls in overly ornate frames. There were piles of rich velvets in every colour imaginable. There were pins in gold and silver, but they were only plain pins. There were stacks of glass sheets in different sizes. And, of course, there were frames from the plain to the regal and faux jewel encrusted like the ones on the walls. There were books on lepidoptery. There were books on how to begin your collection. There were books on the best places to begin collecting the insects. The shop was packed with all the aspiring lepidopterists would need and more.

As Holmes and I strolled along the shop aisles, the proprietor finished assisting a distinguished looking customer and headed our way as the gentleman left the shop. "Why, gentlemen, welcome to my humble shop. How may I be of service to you? Are you beginners or avid collectors?" said the smiling proprietor, Mr. Banks, as the tag read on his shirt.

Holmes turned and spoke first. "We are neither beginners nor avid collectors. A few of our friends collect and we were debating on starting this esteemed hobby, but we thought seeing you first would be most prudent."

"Ah, yes, Mr.???" Banks asked. "Oh, Mr. Rathbone," said Holmes. "My friend here is Mr. Bruce,"

"Well, Mr. Rathbone," said Banks, "there are always beginner books to start you in the right way. I advise those and a butterfly net and a bag to transfer your ladies into." Holmes looked at me briefly after that statement, and I knew he just had to ask....

"Tell me, Mr. Banks, why do you refer to the insects as ladies?"

"Well, Mr. Rathbone," Banks began, "they are resplendent in finery with their colours. Even the moths are, though, more drab. I guess that's why all we collectors do that in working on our hobby," he finished.

"Ah," said Holmes as he walked over to the boxes of pins. He pulled the pin he found in the alley out from his inside pocket and took it from the glassine envelope. The top still looked like it had a drop of blood on it but after cleaning it, we realized the red on the top of the pin was a good quality tiny ruby. "Mr. Banks, I see many lovely kinds of pins but none like this." Holmes then handed the jewelled pin to Mr. Banks.

"Why no. You wouldn't. These are only for the top members in our Leppy Club," said Banks, handing the pin back to Holmes and suddenly turning to walk away, reluctantly hesitant to speak to us.

"And who might they be, Mr. Banks?" said Holmes more seriously and more loudly. I, at that point, took out my pad and pen to write this information down, however, that was not to be.

"Mr. Rathbone, we value member confidentiality," said Banks brusquely. I cannot possibly give you that information as much as I might like to. These are Lords, Princes, Dukes, members of Parliament, masters of industry, and of our government too that we are talking about here. I cannot, I will not give them to you."

Mr. Banks walked behind his counter and pretended to be looking at some books he was pricing and busying himself.

"Holmes hesitated for only a moment. He needed that member's list. Should he blow his cover and risk members finding out, or take this as a loss for now?" Holmes looked Banks directly in his eyes.

"Mr. Banks, are the club meetings held here?" Banks said that where club meetings were held was only known to club members.

Holmes continued, "I can see the indents of several or more four legged chairs right through this door into the other room on the plush rug there." Mr. Banks' eyes widened. "My friend and I will wait until the next meeting, obviously held here, if we have to stand outside your shop every day to see not only who the members are but to ask them who had lost their specially made pin. Since you sell none on your shop floor, I presume they are special orders for the group. I am also guessing they are expensive. I will then proceed to accost them in the street until I can return the pin to its owner. Then I will explain why I had to embarrass them in public instead of finding them discreetly at their club, or even possibly, their home!"

Mr. Banks was sweating profusely and wringing his hands when Holmes finished with him. I had to look down at my shoes in order not to smile and break the mood Holmes had created.

"Mr. Rathbone, please, I misunderstood you. I assumed you would bother them for a reward. Now I see you only want the pin given to its rightful owner. I will write the names down for you. There are only seven board members. They each have the entire club roster. Together they run the club as its board. They do give out the pins as gifts. Several of our members have them, but they will know who has lost one. We meet on Saturday nights at 7 pm."

Banks then grabbed a sheaf of white paper and began writing furiously. When he was finished, he sealed the list in a white envelope and handed it to Holmes. We thanked him, bade him good day and under that same tinkle of bells, we left.

Holmes flagged the third cab, which happened to be a growler. Once we were sitting comfortably inside, he ripped the envelope open. The first name on the list was Mycroft Holmes! After a sudden tap on the roof, Holmes shouted out to the driver, "the Diogenes Club." And we were off.

Chapter 13

The Diogenes

Holmes was silent and deep in thought throughout the entire ride to the Diogenes Club. He stormed out of the cab and left me to pay. I caught up to him at the door of the club as it was opening to let a club patron leave. He pushed past the patron and the poor man in charge of the door, yelling aloud for his brother the entire time.

Now, as you know, speaking was prohibited at the Diogenes. It was a club created to let those averse to conversation and people have a place to go to be with their own thoughts. All this yelling Holmes was doing upset the entire club and men were shushing and storming off in different directions all around us.

Eventually, Mycroft, in all his rotundity, came out from behind a door and grabbed his brother dragging him into the Stranger's Room, the only place where speaking was allowed. I quietly followed them in.

Mycroft sat in total silence and watched Holmes pace back and forth in front of his desk. I sat in a corner chair, unobtrusively, I hoped. Holmes stopped and stood directly in front of Mycroft, staring at him with his grey eyes blazing. "Why have you never told me you were into lepidoptery? I spoke to you not two days ago about the disappearances of women in Whitechapel and all I knew surrounding it, including the lepidoptery aspect, in the hope you could help, but you remained silent. SILENT!"

Holmes placed his hands on the desk in front of Mycroft and lowered his face to look directly into his brother's eyes. "WHY?" he shouted. Holmes then stood and moved a chair directly in front of Mycroft's desk and sat, staring intently at his brother in stony silence.

No one spoke. I sat listening to my own breath and the almost silent ticking of the elegant grandfather clock in the corner of the room. Each inhale and exhale of my breath seemed to shudder in my ears. The younger Holmes finally spoke first, breaking the metronomic madness in my head.

"Mycroft, I let you keep me out of the Ripper case because you knew I had already solved it. I agreed that speaking the truth could hurt 'Queen and Country'. But I regret that now. I will not do it a second time. Not even for you. I will not put Flora in danger. I know it is coming for her. I will solve this case and do so quite publicly. Queen, country and you be damned!"

Mycroft steepled his fingers in the same way Holmes did. He closed his eyes and sighed, then he spoke. "I had hoped to find the answer to this before you realized my connection. But I have not. I don't know who it is. I'm not sure his name is on that list. Even if it was, we are only together for lepidoptery. No one is even allowed to speak of anything else to protect any secrets we might know."

I opened my eyes in shock. Neither Holmes nor I had mentioned a list to Mycroft. The elder Holmes turned and looked at me.

"Yes, Doctor Watson, I know you and my brother have a list you gathered from Mr. Banks in the shop on Oxford Street. It's the only way both of you would find your way here, along with my brother's rage."

Holmes, having enough of his brother's small talk, raised his hands and slammed them down on the desk. He uttered one word to Mycroft, "EXPLAIN!"

Chapter 14

Mycroft Explains

Mycroft gave a shuddering sigh and began. "Once you told me what happened to Miss James and made me privy to your investigation so far, I realized I could eventually be found in a position of compromise. You would connect the investigation to the Leppy Club soon. I immediately began going through the list the board has of all club members because, as you have already realized, those pins were sometimes given as gifts to any of the members, not just the seven board members.

I crossed off dead members, members on extended trips abroad, and members who have had injuries that would prevent them from being suspected. There are forty three remaining members. Of those, there are six bankers, four shipping magnates, thirteen barristers, sixteen members of Parliament who are Lords all, and four government officials, myself included.

I hope you know, brother mine, that I am innocent of all this. However, the public might not have your generosity of spirit, nor would the Crown if my name were to be made public. So far, your friends at the Yard have not let much of this get out, unlike the last little fiasco where the public knew more than the police. But that can change at any moment. Sherlock, you must solve this, and soon."

Mycroft sat back in his chair, pushed a button, and a valet entered. "Food and drink and leave it on a cart outside the door." He cast a look toward his brother. "For God's sake, do not knock."

Holmes, the younger, now steepled his hands for a moment. The room was quiet, and Holmes showed no sign of moving. I knew, however, that his mind was parsing several things at once, pushing some things aside and adding more just as quickly. It was the way his mind palace worked when he was trying to make sense of things and reach conclusions.

There was a soft tinkling outside the door and Mycroft asked me if I could bring the cart in. I did so and pulled it next to his desk. He asked if I would be mother and pour the tea. I agreed. Along with the tea, there were cakes and sandwiches and three shots of brandy. I took my tea and sat back down. I did not pour tea for Holmes, but I did put a brandy on the desk in front of him. Mycroft had a plate piled with sandwiches and cake. He began eating and I sipped my tea.

About twenty minutes later, Holmes reached out, drank the brandy, and put the glass silently back down on the desk. He asked me to take notes. I'm never without my writing book and my pen. I learned that early on. I got them at the ready now.

Holmes began. "There will be two lists. One list we will give to the police. The shipping people, bankers, and barristers. We in this room will take the Lord's and the government officials, excluding Mycroft." Mycroft gave a nod of thanks to Holmes. "I've no doubt that some we are looking for will be in the groups we will assign to the Yard, but we will hopefully have answers from the guilty parties in our groups before they get that far. I suggest we begin immediately with our group and inform Lestrade and Gregson in the morning about what we have found out. I will send them the names in their groups this evening. They can think of plausible lies to tell their superiors and underlings. Both will do exactly that because they helped me solve the Ripper case but were told to forget what they knew. They are men of their word. I trust them. This time the truth will come out and when we want it to. And Mycroft, brother mine, this will come out." Mycroft nodded in the affirmative.

Holmes stood and looked directly at his brother behind the desk. "Mycroft, if you ever lie to me or omit the truth from me again, you will no longer have a brother. I make a hell of an enemy. Do I make myself clear on that point?" Mycroft, caught with almost a whole slice of cake in his mouth, just nodded his agreement. With that, Holmes grabbed his hat and coat and walked out, leading me to do the same. The doorman had a hansom already at the curb as he was probably waiting to see the back end of us.

The Keeper of the Flame

Well, this was unexpected. That whore Mary was now living under the roof of 'the' Sherlock Holmes, Consulting Detective. My spy said he saw her and that doctor go to her old apartment, where I was hoping to apprehend her, and collect her things. So, who is it then that she is bedding? Holmes or Watson? Maybe both. She's done two before. She's done more than two before. No matter. She is MY whore, MY moth, and I shall snatch her back and pin her to my board again.

The moths we have collected so far are behaving splendidly. They want their opium. So easy to addict a whore. I added my special mix into the opium. A potent aphrodisiac, cocaine, and a bit of morphine for the pain our clients make them endure. They become agreeable moths who will gladly suffer any degradation and pain to keep getting their opium, just like my moth did several years ago and will again.

I've created a club for men who are like me. Men who don't hold this new belief that women can be equal to men. Women are subservient! We hold the belief that women were created to serve us in any and every way we wish, whenever we wish it!

It was easy, to begin with moths, they are so compliant and willing to please. After all, they are whores. Ah, but I do believe I mentioned my sister. My dear darling sister who also wouldn't do a woman's job of helping her brother get off. It's not like I wanted to take her virginity, there were other ways she could have serviced me. She was, after all, my sister. But she eventually forced me to take her virginity to show her the error of her ways. A man can only take so much. We need release and women, all women, were created to provide it, including my stupid sister.

I took my sister long enough and hard enough to make sure no man would ever mistake her for a virgin on her wedding night. Then I found the most lustful, violent, and debauched friend I had, a barrister, and married her off to him. Our parents were both dead these three years, thankfully, and there were no other relatives. She had no one to protect her. I bet she doesn't say no now.

It was she, well her behaviour, who gave me the idea to expand the club to butterflies as well. A club where men of my class can bring their wives to, shall we say, learn more skills for the bedroom. They would be taught their lessons by all of us taking turns bedding them, so there was no excuse for them not to learn.

No opium for the butterflies. No, our butterflies would be given laudanum, the more respectable version of the drug. Just enough to addict them and encourage them to learn the proper way to service their husbands, and any other women or men their husbands might bring to the bedroom, without complaint and with obedience. If they didn't learn, there were always more lessons after all. Moth lessons.

So now I need a plan to get my Mary back. My moth. And I'll kill anyone who tries to stop me. Man or woman. Who knows, maybe I'll do her and her friend Rose together. I bet they'd like that. You know how women lie about wanting sex with other women. And I'll make Sherlock Holmes and Doctor Watson watch us.

Chapter 15

The Suspects

We arrived at Baker Street, and Holmes went directly into the bedroom where Flora was resting to tell her what we had learned at the shop on Oxford Street and the matter of the Diogenes Club. I heard her raised voice and wondered if Holmes really had any clue about how his life had changed by falling in love. It gave me a nice chuckle.

However, they came out of the bedroom arm in arm, and Holmes went to his chair and picked up a pipe and his Persian slipper. Flora went downstairs and returned a while later with Mrs. Hudson and Billy, along with a tray of sandwiches, slices of cake, and coffee and tea.

Holmes, of course, would not eat. However, I appreciated the fact he had learned to wait until food was present for those of us who did not exist on brain power alone. I pulled out the two lists I had gotten from Mycroft, along with my notes on how they were to be divided and handed them to Holmes. Then I headed for the food to have my fill. I couldn't eat at the Diogenes. The Holmes brothers, in anger, were more than I could take.

Holmes looked to Billy first and bade him to eat his fill. There was a job for him to do. Holmes then turned one list over and began writing on it. When he was finished it was sealed in an envelope and given to Billy with a command to give the envelope only to Lestrade or Gregson post-haste. He tossed him a shilling and handed him some sandwiches and cake he placed in a cloth to give to any other irregulars helping the cause of finding the inspectors tonight. He requested Billy return right after his assignment was finished. Billy was off. Then Holmes requested a cup of tea.

Mrs. Hudson got up and poured the tea for Holmes and then began to clean up the remnants of the meal to bring the trays downstairs. Holmes reached for her wrist gently and bade her to sit down. Then he spoke. "Tonight, Watson and I found out the scope of this case. It is larger than the Ripper case a few years ago. On the list I gave Billy to give to the inspectors were the names of barristers, shipping magnates, and bankers, several of whom own businesses with other well-to-do people. On the list I hold here, there are sixteen members of Parliament, Lords all, and four members of the government in the highest echelons, all of whom mix with the Royals on a regular basis. These lists are our suspects."

Mrs. Hudson's cup clattered as she placed it in her saucer. Holmes looked at her to see if she was all right, then he continued. "Our lists will overlap. Mycroft and I are sure about it. Flora is as well. This means I will need help from all of you. There are too many suspects and not enough of us or the police. Mrs. Hudson, if you will accept the danger of this case..." Mrs. Hudson stopped

Holmes by reaching her hand out and shaking it in the air. She looked at Holmes, then she spoke. "You and Doctor Watson are my boys. Now I have a girl, the lovely and brave Flora. Sherlock, you know my past. I would be delighted to help in any way possible. Women stick together. Women protect each other. And mostly, we are strong. We are willing to fight for beliefs, loved ones, and truth. Yes, Sherlock. I will help in any way I can." Holmes got up and embraced her and said, "ah, Mrs. Hudson. I can always count on you." Flora then embraced Mrs. Hudson as she sat back on the sofa with her.

Holmes then stood and walked over to his chalkboards. He rubbed his hands together and looked at us. "Well, are we ready to begin?" Holmes looked at Flora with an understanding of what was to come and said to her, "would you like to speak first?"

Chapter 16

Flora's Big Reveal

Flora stood up and begged everyone's attention for a moment before Holmes began to delve into his plans for this case with us. She explained she wanted Mrs. Hudson and me to know exactly who she was. I looked at Mrs. Hudson quizzically, and she shrugged her shoulders, indicating this was new to her as well. Holmes, she said, already knew what she was about to tell us. "I'm sorry I didn't tell you sooner but telling Sherlock was difficult enough, and I knew I didn't have the strength of mind to tell this secret again for a while. Both of you know how and why I became an unfortunate before the time of the Ripper. You also know how those wonderful women helped me after the ripping stopped. But you don't know that I had a room in Whitechapel at that time. I was off opium by then and was at odds with where my life was going and what I was going to do. I had to sell my body for food and to pay for my room, but that left barely enough for anything else. Though I wanted to change, I had no way, no money, and no idea how to make it happen.

At the time I was going through all this in my mind, a sweet and young girl came into my small world. She was made unfortunate when her family abandoned her in London with nothing after it came to be known to them that she had slept with her intended before

UNDER THE PALE YELLOW STREET LAMP

marriage. She had been selling her body for months before I met her. Her name was Flora James." Mrs. Hudson's hand flew to her mouth, and she made a soft, strangled cry. Watson stood and shouted, "WHAT?!"

Holmes bade us to be calm and listen to the rest of Flora's story. Though we were now in shock, we sent our attention back to her. She was sitting now, and Holmes had placed his hand protectively on her shoulder. Flora continued. "As I was saying, I met Flora James as she was trying to get a doss for the night. I let her stay with me. It became a pattern that when she was unable to find or pay for a doss, she would find me and if I was not engaged with a client in my room…,"

Suddenly, Flora dipped her head as though the words pained her to speak them, and Mrs. Hudson and I could see she was struggling to continue. Holmes poured her a brandy and bade her to drink. After a few sips and words of encouragement from Holmes, Flora began again. "She stayed with me on a regular basis on and off. After two women had been brutally ripped in one night, I had a few of the girls stay in my room for safety. The landlord saw us and threw them out. Only one in a room being paid rent for only one, he said. So, when Flora came, I tried to stay out most of the night and earn so she could use the room and sleep, and in turn, we would have food in the morning from my earnings, and I could sleep as she went out in the safety of daylight.

But one night, after becoming so tired, I headed home only to find inspector Abberline and half of Scotland Yard in my room. I tried to get closer to see what had happened. When I did, I bent over and retched. Flora had been ripped, and her body lay scattered all over my bed and everything in my room. The police already had a name. Mary Kelly, me. I was now dead. I didn't go up to the inspector or his men. I walked away, knowing I could never be in that room again. Mary Kelly was dead. But Flora James lived again. In me." Flora put her head in her hands and wept. Holmes was kneeling before her and holding her gently, whispering softly in her ear.

Mrs. Hudson and I were sitting as if in a daze, and we were struck quite speechless. Finally, I got up and said, "Flora, you are braver than I ever knew. You gave your friend a great honor and a loving way to let her live on in your heart." I sat feeling a bit choked up myself. With my few words said, I quietly pushed back in my chair.

Mrs. Hudson got up and encircled both Holmes and Flora in her arms. "Thank God you are still here for us, Flora. You have made Sherlock a better man. You have graced me as a daughter in my home. The two of you have both suffered, but now you will heal each other, and your lives will go on, and so will countless others as you use your great minds and hearts to help them. You both have a gift. Now you both have love." Mrs. Hudson stood and went to her seat while pulling a handkerchief from her pocket and dabbing at her eyes. I poured a small brandy for each of us. And Holmes refocused us back to the business at hand.

Chapter 17

The Sandwich

Holmes, at his board again, with the three of us watching, wrote the names from the lists in proper columns in his impeccable script. He began, "here is the list we have in its entirety. What I need from all of us now is to have everyone delve into my scrapbooks and Debrett's and read everything I have compiled on these people. We need to shorten the lists. We will never find ways to interview or follow everyone. There is a risk that we might eliminate the person or persons we are looking for, but if we are all attentive, the risk is small. Once we have accomplished that, then we can formulate the next steps. I have written much of the same on the back of the inspectors' lists. They will know whom they can eliminate, leaving a list of those that they must see in person to be eliminated. Shall we get started?"

Flora and I went for Holmes' books, and Mrs. Hudson cleaned the table and surrounding area so what we needed could be piled close to the chairs. Holmes crossed Mycroft off the board and took his seat, and lit a pipe. He said, "we all need to read everything on each name, and we will discuss whether they are to be eliminated or not." He read the first name, and we began.

After the first two hours, we stood to stretch, and Mrs.

Hudson fetched tea and some shortbread biscuits she had made that morning. We discussed three people and could easily eliminate two of them. We had sixteen to go. We began again in the pattern of reading two or three and discussing them. We watched the darkness overtake London, and the streetlights sparkled like stars. Holmes refreshed the fire, and Mrs. Hudson and Flora went to fetch a late dinner of cold sandwiches so we could continue our work.

I wondered how far the inspectors had gotten with their list. It was longer than ours, but I felt sure they had their own 'books' on the people on that list and were probably familiar with some in the police sense. They were due to meet with us at 8 AM. Holmes was not worried if they still had people left to vet on their list. He said our list would hold the master key, and the other keys would be known by that.

We ate the wonderful turkey, stuffing, and cranberry sauce sandwiches which had a gravy-soaked piece of bread in the centre. The sandwiches were so good they deserved a name. I kept a hand over mine so no one would be tempted to steal it! Then we began again. We continued until dawn, then left to get a couple of hours of sleep. Holmes, even with Flora's coaxing, would not sleep.

Chapter 18
Maybe Better off Dead

When we awoke, it was to Mrs. Hudson's delicious scones and clotted cream with strawberry jam. A generous-sized teapot sat steaming and scenting the room with the citrus aroma of Earl Grey. The board was finished. Holmes had completed it in the night. He then woke Mrs. Hudson and helped her with the breakfast feast. He was, I think, definitely a changed man now. I reminded myself to thank Flora for that. Often.

As we ate, we looked at the completed list. All other names were now gone. We had one government official and six Lords, all with special positions in Parliament that had them interacting with the Royal Family daily. That did not bode well. After finishing up our food, Mrs. Hudson cleaned the table and put a warm towel over the pile of scones still left. Holmes began his discussion of the list.

"These are the six Lords and singular government official left. It is a list we can work with. All four of us will be vetting these people in person in various guises. If my theory is correct, all of them play a part in these abductions. If I'm right, at least a third of the inspectors' list as well."

I took a sip of tea to wash down the final bite of my scone and asked, "how can that be? I can see two, maybe three, to abduct the women, but it's overkill with all the rest. Do you think they are taking turns?"

"Ah, Watson. You look, but you do not see. Have we found a single body, or body part, of any of these women? No. They are alive, and they are being held somewhere. That must mean there is a purpose. If you are abducting unfortunates, what do you think the purpose might be?"

Flora gasped. "Oh, Sherlock, no, these poor women are being held for sex. Surely these men can pay the little unfortunates ask for, and the brothels are not expensive for these men as they pay most of the madams for repeated use. How can this be? Do they believe it should be free?" She thought for a minute. Her mind worked almost as quickly as Holmes'. "No! They are making them sex slaves. Taking these women over and over until they die!" She put a hand to her eyes and cried softly. Mrs. Hudson went to her and put an arm about her in a motherly fashion.

"Flora, my love," said Sherlock, "it's much worse than that. There are men, sadly even from the upper classes, who need to physically dominate a woman in rough and painful ways in order to complete the sex act. I'm afraid this is what is happening now. And soon, if we don't stop them, it is my belief they intend to bring their wives, the 'butterflies', there to learn how to submit to these acts to please them in the bedroom as well. The moths and the butterflies will suffer great pain unless they are stopped."

Mrs. Hudson turned an angry shade of red. She was shaking and looked at Holmes. "Sherlock, you know my story. You know I've killed before. Though I vowed not to take a life ever again, I will. Tell me what to do. I will do anything. For these poor women, I will kill again. I want to be part of this in every way."

I spoke next. "Holmes is correct. It seems this is the probable answer. As a physician, I have seen women who were treated like this. Yes, many were unfortunates who angered a pimp or were asked by those who could not pay but did the act anyway and in a rough and cruel manner. But I have seen many upper-class women who married sexual deviants who like to inflict as much pain as possible during sex. The scars were awful and many of these women were left sterile or worse. We must act with all that is in our power to save these women. And we must make an example of these men to prevent others like them from pursuing their terrible ways."

There was a knock on the downstairs door. Billy opened it, and we heard him send the inspectors up.

Chapter 19

The Suspects ... Again

The inspectors doffed coats and hats and found seats. Mrs. Hudson would not let us begin again until the inspectors were fed the warm scones washed down by Earl Grey tea that she had saved for them. Meanwhile, Holmes had taken the shortened list from Lestrade and was adding the names to the other chalkboard. Soon, we were all settled and directed our attention to Holmes.

Holmes called on Lestrade to explain how his list was shortened. Lestrade spoke, "Gregson and I split the list. We found out that all but one of the shipping magnates had been on extended time out of the country. We have two bankers who were here, and we have records on them both for previous drunken and lewd behaviours. Finally, seven barristers remain on the list. The others were dedicated family men out on the continent with their families for most of the time since this debacle began.". He sat back down, and Holmes flipped the board to our side.

"As you can see, we have six Lords and one government official on our list. Between both lists, we have gone from forty-three to seventeen. Still a lot of suspects, but they are certainly more manageable than forty-three. I am assuming we will find most of our suspects know each other or are connected in some way. Several of

71

them are the same age. We need backgrounds on all of them. For this part, I have gone to my brother Mycroft. He owes me favours for a lifetime. Once we have backgrounds and can make some connections between these men, we can decide how the investigation will proceed. We will probably need all of them followed for at least a day or two. That will give Mycroft a chance to compile the dossiers if he hasn't done so already and give us a way we might catch one of them in the act of abducting a woman or leading us to the location of the woman. We need to decide who follows whom because we will begin tonight.

Lestrade said he could spare ten men for two nights, and together we determined he would keep with his list of the magnate, the bankers, and the barristers. It would be easier to keep the Lords and the government official out of the public eye if it became known people were being followed for ties to the disappearances of women in Whitechapel if we were doing the following. Lestrade and Gregson left after strongly admonishing us to follow only, no engagement, and to maintain our safety above all. We took a break after that to see to our needs and refreshments for anyone wanting some more to eat.

Chapter 20
The Final List

Holmes was seated in his chair, I in mine, Flora and Mrs. Hudson sat on the sofa, and Billy had come upstairs and sat in the barrel chair. Holmes had arranged for the irregulars to assist us, and Billy would disperse their marching orders along with the appropriate coins.

The board looked like this:

Brigadier Charles Smith, Lord Reginald Dell,

Lord Johnathan Drake, Lord William Frake,

Lord Robert Hutchens, Lord Scott Killian,

Lord Thomas Ledingford

Holmes had worked out our schedules when we absented ourselves to take our earlier break. Now he explained all of it to us. "I am assigning the Brigadier to Mrs. Hudson. He lives nearby the Diogenes and works in Mycroft's offices. Mycroft will have eyes on him during the day. My dear Mrs. Hudson, I would like you to get to know the Brigadier. There is a late dinner this evening at the Brigadier's house, and you will be going as Mycroft's guest. Please speak to him. Do not reveal your address is 221b. But keep to the truth about your life. Change names and events as you see fit but stick as close to the truth as possible. Ask him about his family, his hobbies, and his other activities when the opportunity presents itself.

I know you can handle him." Mrs. Hudson smiled and shook her head yes.

Holmes continued, "Billy, divide your groups into three units of three. One to watch, one to find me or Watson, and one to accompany the one who stayed in case your target moves. Then once he stops, one of you can run to find myself or Watson. Do not, and I repeat, do not engage with the person you are following. These are dangerous men. Stay until all the lights in their homes go out, then you are done until tomorrow night. Billy, do you understand me?" Billy repeated all Holmes had told him. "Now," said Holmes, "here are your shillings. Divide them equally with your teams. Here are the three papers with the names and addresses. Get some sleep in the bedroom Mrs. Hudson has provided for you after you have chosen and informed your teams and tell them to sleep as well. Off with you." Billy scooped up the coins and the papers and ran down the stairs and out the door.

Holmes stood by the chalkboard and wrote irregulars next to Lords Dell, Frake, and Killian. He turned to us and said, "I gave the irregulars these three because they are close to the army barracks by St. James Park. They are in proximity to each other in case one team runs into trouble. I don't foresee that happening, but I prefer they have options if it does.

Now, Watson, you will be watching Lord Drake. Here is the

address. As far as the instructions, watch, follow if need be, leave when the house lights go out and do not engage. My dear Flora, you will follow Lord Hutchens. I will take Lord Ledingford. Now rest. It may be a long night." Holmes handed me one paper, Flora one paper, and he pocketed the other. "Tonight shall be interesting. I predict we will run across each other as well as Lestrade's and Gregson's men over the next few nights. Be prepared for that". Holmes then went to his chair and picked out a pipe.

Chapter 21

A Christmas Wish

After everything was cleaned and quiet now, Flora was standing by the window overlooking Baker Street. It was the end of the second week of November. The chill in London was apparent. Frost was on the edges of the window. Soon there will be snow and Christmas and the New Year. All Flora could think about was her friend Rose and the other poor women this fiend had taken. She saw me approach her in the window's reflection. She turned to me. "Doctor Watson, do you think there is a possibility we will find the women before Christmas? Christmas needs to be with friends and family. While these women do not have much in the way of either, they always have the Christmas spirit. I'd like them to be able to hold to the little things we used to do at Christmas time. Do you know we always found little things to give each other or do for each other on Christmas? A boiled sweet, a sliver of soap, a part of a comb. We all saved up something, and we always made sure everyone in our crowd had something too. What I want to give them this year is their freedom from this fiend."

I was touched by Flora's heartfelt speech, and ashamed. I had so much more than these women and sometimes so much less Christmas spirit. I hesitated but a moment because I had an idea.

"Flora, do you want to drive by our Lord's homes and reconnoitre? We could then have a quick lunch and come back home to rest for this evening."

"Doctor Watson, that would be wonderful. I get to go out again, and I'll feel better prepared if I know where I'm to go. A nice meal with you will be a bonus. I know Sherlock will not move from his chair except maybe to play his Stradivarius to help himself think, then smoke his pipe some more. I am used to spending much of my time outside. While I like the warmth I've become accustomed to, I will like being outside tonight." She turned and made a small wincing sound. "Oh, these stitches pull so much now. They hinder my movements."

"Flora, would you like me to remove them before we leave? There could be a bit of bleeding, and I will bandage those areas, but you are healed enough for them to be removed." I suddenly found two arms around me and Flora whispering in my ear, "Doctor Watson, if I wasn't already madly in love with Sherlock, I'd love you!" With that, she kissed my cheeks, leaving me blushing like a schoolboy. She ran into Holmes' bedroom with my medical bag in hand. As I went to follow her, I heard Holmes whisper, "Watson, she's spoken for." I chuckled. Jealousy. Holmes was indeed becoming more human.

The Keeper of the Flame

I'm so close to my Mary now. I can sometimes see her in the window of 221b Baker Street. Just seeing her makes me understand that I will indeed get her back. She is mine. I remember taking her that first time. The look in her eyes when she realized I had taken from her what she could only give once. She tried to fight back, but she was too drugged. It was intoxicating to stare into those pained eyes. I look forward to seeing those pained eyes again. Very pained.

I've improved the drug mix I use. My moths are more aware, more participatory, and more fun. My friends and I have all learned and studied before we 'set up shop,' shall we say? I learned from the ripper case that to hide in plain sight is to literally get away with murder. It's easy to catch my moths. To hide my moths too. But why kill a perfectly good whore. Using them brutally is so much more fun. Uncle Jack, you should have listened to me. When he came to me that night and said he killed my Mary. I had to kill him. I used his ruby-hilted knife. The one I lost in Mary's side. I now know he didn't kill her, but it was his time anyway. Sherlock Holmes and his bunch knew who he was.

My best friend from university, Lord William Frake, came up with the idea to start a different kind of lepidoptery collection. one of the moths, the whores of London, and the butterflies, the married ladies of London. This collection would not be pinned on a board. *Oh no, this collection, both moths and butterflies, was made to be played with and used. William and I have the same taste in women. He is like a brother to me. He had my Mary after I was finished using her body that first time we played with our first moth, Mary.*

But it was two of our friends, Brigadier Charles Smith and his banker Sir Allen Best who helped us monetize our club and were key in the expansion to other countries. Dues in our club were high, but in exchange, you had free reign of what you did to the moths and butterflies. You could even pull off their wings if you like. But there's a hefty fee for that, and you must dispose of it properly. No one has killed a moth yet, or a butterfly, but some of us can be quite brutal in our fun. Even deadly. It's just a matter of time.

An endeavour like ours was tried a few years ago but failed. They took children for their sex slaves. I'm not so bad now, am I? I thought not. If you take children, you get Scotland Yard on you quickly. But who cares about whores? Certainly, the police didn't care about Jack's escapades. He knew they wouldn't. As you now know, they did catch him. Well, it wasn't their brainless lot. Sherlock Holmes did but never was allowed to participate in the investigation, take credit, or talk about it. Why, you ask? Come now, even you aren't that stupid. He was one of us. Untouchable. And as for butterflies, well, our wives are our property to do with as we wish without worrying about the law.

Ah, I must leave you now. My moth is about to leave her place of safety. Mary, can you feel me watching you? Soon you will be mine again.

Chapter 22

Take the 3rd Cab Watson

I successfully removed Flora's stitches. A few were tender and needed bandaging, but she will need to move freely tonight, and she was so relieved they were gone. She was still dressing, and I left the bedroom to give her privacy.

I went to ask Holmes if he wanted to come with us. He never removed his eyes from the Debrett's and scrapbooks he was reading. There were more of the same strewn about the floor around him. There was a lot about Lord Ledingford and Lord Blackwell. I asked him some questions, and his answers and comments were monosyllabic.

To do you want to go: "No."
To my having taken my firearm: "Webley?" To safety: "Observe."
To time: "Early."

Then Flora exited the bedroom. I helped her on with her wrap and went to fetch a hansom. "Watson!" Holmes yelled. "Do take the third cab." "Of course, Holmes." Flora kissed Holmes goodbye, and we were off.

"What was that about the third cab?" Flora asked as we waited. "Holmes has it in his head that the first cab may be a setup. The second one may be a setup if they think he's deduced the first.

81

But criminals never bother with the third one. He's always been correct on this. Saved our lives a few times and almost cost me mine when I broke it." Watson answered. "Ah, the third cab approaches!" We entered its confines, and we were off on our adventure.

Flora smiled. "What absolutely logical reasoning. His mind is so different from ours. I can apply his methods, and quite successfully, I might add, but to fathom his logical mind, I just cannot." She turned to observe the streets as we made our way to the addresses on both of our papers. I've no doubt that she will memorize every street. I observed that her mind was not as different from his as she thought.

We found that our Lord's homes were not too far from each other. By passing through a lane behind one, we could circle around to the end of the street of the other. There were several spots near both homes that were concealed and would allow for unfettered observation. When we were both satisfied with what we saw and how we would approach this evening, we left for an early lunch at the Criterion.

Chapter 23

A Quieter Sherlock at the Diogenes

As soon as Watson was off with Flora, Sherlock prepared to go out. After choosing a hansom, he told the driver to take him to the Diogenes Club. Upon his arrival, the doorman stepped back with a frightened look on his face. Sherlock stepped forward and said, "I assure you I intend to follow every rule. Please tell my brother I will be waiting quietly in the Stranger's Room for him. I am expected. The man opened the door and allowed Sherlock inside. He spoke to the valet, who went in search of Mycroft as Sherlock found his way to the Stranger's Room quietly. The doorman went back to his duties, thankful the brothers were being civil to each other again.

Sherlock was pacing as Mycroft shuffled his way into the room and took his seat. A house boy with a tea cart followed Mycroft in and left the cart next to the desk. He backed out and closed the door. As the final click of the door sounded, Sherlock asked, "Do you have the information on the seventeen?" Mycroft nodded in the affirmative and began pouring tea. Sherlock took a cup and sat. Mycroft took his tea to his desk and handed Sherlock seventeen folders. Sherlock began to peruse them.

"Brother mine, read those later when you are ensconced in Baker Street waiting for your Flora to come home safely from the

Criterion with the good Doctor Watson. Sherlock's head popped up. Yes, they are being followed. You will understand why in a moment. I will give you the nasty rundown on what we have found and tell you what I think is happening."

Mycroft shifted his weight in the seat, and when comfortable, he began. "These men are all in some type of trouble. The usual drink, drugs, adultery, gambling, and whatever else men get into that can warp their bodies and their minds. We at the Leppy Club knew these men were trouble but it did not affect the club, nor did we realize the extent of their depravity. Why would we? We collected, shared, and told facts about our butterflies and moths. However, as a result of the investigation into the men that you requested, I learned more, much more." Mycroft shuddered in disgust, and his jowls settled last.

"Let us begin with Lord Ledingford. He has a cruel streak. Madams say he hurts their girls to the point of causing damage, sometimes severe and disfiguring. The horrifying physical damage he causes is topped only by the emotional damage he inflicts as well. He does, however, bring his own doctor. The doctor-in-ordinary to the Queen. To tend to the girls." Sherlock stopped glancing at the files and looked up at Mycroft.

"I thought you would like that," said Mycroft as he continued. "He has visited these bordellos with two of the Queen's grandsons and a few cousins to the Queen as well as various Lords on the lists. He also has brought a few lawyer friends, including his personal barrister. All on your list of seventeen. There is also talk he is to marry Princess Alix, God forbid. Oh, and most interesting is that he frequents the bordellos with a few school chums. All Lords on your list, as well as the magnate on the inspectors' list. Though in the last two months, they have hardly graced the bordellos at all. I assume you now know why."

Sherlock stood. "Yes, I had expected as much. I thought we would find them connected. Abhorrent behaviours all Mycroft. They torture these women during sex. Brutally so. Soon, if it hasn't already begun, their wives will be receiving similar treatment to condition them into giving these men the kind of sex they want. If we cannot stop them, many women will suffer and surely die. And what of your government agent?"

"Ah, Brigadier Charles Smith," said Mycroft. "He is a cagey one. Has had a half dozen meetings we know about with Ledingford and a banker and a few of the barristers from the inspectors' list. When he comes back to his office, he pulls charts from the middle east, the southern states in America, and the southern Russian border. Seems to be looking for remote properties with street access and corrupt police or military in the area." Mycroft stopped to sip his tea.

"Sherlock, you realize we are seeing the beginning of a sex trafficking ring like the one recently stopped by the metropolitan police that trafficked children. I think they are going to capture and drug more women and traffic them to these places to set up shop like they have in London. We are fortunate enough to see the ground level of this business, so to speak. We must stop them. I will contact my people in these countries and see how far they have gotten. And one more thing I think you will find most interesting."

Sherlock looked at his brother, still reeling from the depravity of these men. Mycroft said, "you told me Flora's story. Who she really is, or should I say, was. When I investigated Ledingford's background, I found out he has a sister about Flora's age. She's married now to the vilest barrister; he's on our list, who has had multiple arrests for physical depravity to women, especially unfortunates. He keeps getting the charges dropped. Anyway, the sister had a friend. A servant girl named Mary Kelly who disappeared during the same time Flora said she was kidnapped and drugged by her friend's brother. Ledingford and his cronies are the ones who kidnapped, raped, addicted her to drugs, and sold her to a brothel. This now, of course, creates a problem."

Sherlock sat stock still in his chair. He was processing what his brother had just told him. His face went through several contortions of emotions and settled on anger. He gripped the arms of the chair with his long fingers. He stayed that way for several minutes. Then his body relaxed, and he spoke. "Mycroft, this does present a slight problem and a change in our plans. Flora needs to be told all of this. And who Ledingford really is, the least of them. She will need to come to terms with all of it and either absent herself from the investigation or continue with it on my terms. I believe she will continue. She is, as Doctor Watson says, a lot like me."

Sherlock continued, "If we are lucky, we will find where the women are being held and remove them to medical treatment before anyone is the wiser, but it's never that easy. That is just the beginning. We will need all the men arrested and charged. We can't do this piecemeal by arresting the men who happen to be in attendance when we rescue the women and hoping to have them testify about each other. They are cowards. They will not do that. They have the money to disappear. We will need to change our plans. I will inform the irregulars who will start tonight at Lord Ledingford's home. That is where I'm sure we will find the women. I will work with Lestrade and Gregson and the Yard to come up with a plan to free the women and arrest as many of the men at one time as we can. Mycroft, will you please see how far their overseas plans have progressed as soon as possible? That may complicate things. There are others that may need prosecution. Finally, I will tell Flora when she comes home. I fear I have the most difficult part of these plans."

"Sherlock," said Mycroft looking at his brother, "I haven't

finished. Brace yourself for this. Ledingford is a recent name for the Lord. His name was changed a few years ago. It was to protect his family. After all, he had a younger sister to protect at that time. His name was Lord Thomas Blackwell. He became that after his father, then his uncle died. Thomas is Jack the Ripper's nephew."

Sherlock looked to the floor and sighed. Then he pulled himself together, thanked his brother, and left the room, closing the door softly without another word.

Chapter 24

Sherlock Gets Busy

Sherlock left the Diogenes Club with a heavy heart and a determined mind. He found Billy first. He explained the change of plans and that they will all watch Lord Ledingford's home and report to him who visits over the next two nights. Billy agreed to inform the others and that they will begin after dinner. Mrs. Hudson, Billy said, had offered to feed all of them before they left this evening. Billy would show the photos and sketches of the people they were looking for that Sherlock had compiled to the other irregulars while they were at 221b. Though most could recognize half the people in London! The irregulars were impressive and bright children.

Then Sherlock went to Scotland Yard and met with Lestrade and Gregson. He showed them the seventeen files and briefed them on what he had learned from Mycroft. Gregson would get a detail of men in plainclothes to watch Lord Ledingford's home for the next two nights to assist the irregulars. Gregson could then use them as messengers between him and Scotland Yard and Sherlock and Watson too. Lestrade would contact the foreign police as Mycroft had already contacted the overseas government authorities. Then he would meet Sherlock, Watson, Mrs. Hudson, and Flora to plan for the rescue of the women two nights from now. He'd pull from the Metropolitan Police if he was short personnel. Further afield if necessary.

Finally, Sherlock headed home to get a brief rest before Flora and Watson returned. He knew telling Flora would be hard. Flora had so locked that part of her life away that he wasn't sure telling her wouldn't traumatize her beyond the ability to function. When she found out who Ledingford really was, it would be an even harder blow. However, he was counting on her strength and her love of these women to help her get through the pain he knew he would cause her tonight. Then, he was going to ask her to do something unbelievably difficult. He would have Mrs. Hudson in the room with him for that part. Of course, Watson would be on standby for all of them. Watson, the backbone of almost every investigation since they met that morning in St. Bart's. Watson, his Boswell. His friend. His one friend.

Chapter 25

Flora Knows the Enemy

When I arrived at 221b, I found Mrs. Hudson in my room tidying up for tonight. I sat her down and explained the plans had changed for all but her, and why. Mrs. Hudson had seen and done more things than people would guess upon meeting her. Not even Watson knew what crime she was forced to commit and why. I had helped her and we bonded like mother and son. I explained what I would be asking of Flora and of her too, and she patted my hand and said Flora is much stronger than I realized and that the two of them, she and Flora, would execute their rolls perfectly. I hoped I wasn't doing something horribly wrong, sending the two women I love best in the world into the lion's den. I told her I would be resting until Flora and Watson returned.

About two hours later, I heard Watson returning home with Flora. They were chatting amiably as they walked up the 17 steps. When they entered, followed quietly behind by Mrs. Hudson, they saw the table set for two with tea and biscuits laid out beautifully. The fire was blazing, and candlelight flickered softly upon the crystal holders on the table's center, creating a magical effect. Mrs. Hudson quietly took Doctor Watson's arm and led him silently back downstairs. I had arranged this earlier with Mrs. Hudson. I asked her to tell Doctor Watson about the change in plans and what Mycroft had found out, and I would find some way to tell Flora without traumatizing her further. Mrs. Hudson gladly agreed.

I helped Flora remove her woolen and silk wraps. Once they were hung, I took her arm and walked her to her chair, pulling it out and then pushing it in gently as she sat down. Once she was seated, I sat in my own chair and looked at her across the table in the glow of the candles. She was beautiful, my Flora. Her dark hair was partially pulled up and tied with a velvet ribbon in a true navy blue. Wisps of her wavy hair had escaped and now were in gentle waves around her face. Her well-tailored outfit, a navy and pink tweed, looked impeccable. The dark navy suited her porcelain skin; the pink made her glow. They were her favourite colours. The candlelight made her blue eyes sparkle, and her skin looked luminous. I was mesmerized and momentarily unable to proceed. She returned my gaze with a quizzical look. I began before I could change my mind, "Flora, there has been a necessary change of plans."

Flora was a bit taken aback. "Sherlock, tell me what has happened. Please." She reached across the table and placed her hand over mine. I raised it to my lips and kissed the soft skin. Flora knew something was very wrong. I was obviously stalling. She stood and went around the table to me, and I rose to meet her. "Sherlock, please tell me what has happened. Has a body been found? Was another woman abducted? You are scaring me."

I wrapped my arms around her, and she held me back. I could smell the carnation perfume she wore, Jicky, a gift from me. I could feel her heart beating against me. I knew I needed to tell her, but I couldn't bear hurting her. This information would do just that. For the first time in my adult life I, 'Sherlock Holmes, consulting detective,' was scared.

I led her to the sofa, where we both sat. I held her hands in mine, and I quietly spoke. "Mycroft compiled dossiers on the seventeen people on our list. He finished it in a few hours and not a few days like I had anticipated. There was one who had a new lordship name change bestowed on him only a few years ago. His name was not always Lord Thomas Ledingford. His name prior was Sir Thomas Blackwell."

I felt Flora's hands begin to tremble. Soon her whole body was shaking. Feeling helpless, I went to hold her, but she stood up. She walked only a few steps and collapsed on the floor in a heap of navy and pink. I knelt beside her and scooped her into my arms. I held her limp body against my chest. I buried my face in her hair and whispered, "I'm so sorry, my love." Then…I, the great Sherlock Holmes, consulting detective, cried.

Chapter 26

Blackwell

Hearing a crash from above, Mrs. Hudson and I dropped the biscuits we were eating, flew up the 17 steps, and opened the door wide. We both stopped dead still at the sight before us. Holmes was holding a limp Flora with his head buried in her hair. Hearing us, he looked up, and we saw his eyes red and tear-stained.

Fearing the worst, I ran to Flora and tried to check her pulse. What I could feel was slow but strong. Mrs. Hudson went to Holmes and was trying to pull him away so I could examine Flora in more depth. She was cooing to him gently, but Holmes would not release Flora. He held her tighter as if to impart his strength into her. I placed an arm around him and, speaking very much man to man; I asked him to lay her back on the floor, so I could examine her while he stayed there to see if she needed further attention. He then released her quite gently onto the floor.

I was retaking Flora's pulse as she began to come around. Her first word was 'Sherlock,' and he reached out and helped her sit up. After a few moments, she indicated toward the sofa, and Holmes gently helped Flora stand and walk back to her seat on the sofa.

She sat against a pillow, and Holmes covered her with a quilt, and she lay back and took a deep breath as he sat next to her.

Flora looked up at Holmes and wiped his tears with her fingers. Then she said, "Sherlock, do go on. I'm afraid I've rudely interrupted you, and I want to know more. I want to know all of it."

Holmes pulled himself together and asked Mrs. Hudson and me to sit with them. He then explained he had just told Flora who Lord Thomas Ledingford really was when she became upset and fainted. "Forgive me, all of you. I have never had to purposely hurt a woman I was truly in love with before. It's positively horrendous."

Holmes checked to see if Flora needed anything before continuing. "I'm afraid I'm not finished yet. Flora, you could not know this information, but the Jack the Ripper case was solved." Flora gasped, and her hand flew to her throat. "It took Watson, Lestrade, Gregson, Mrs. Hudson, and me to piece it all together. I was not allowed near the case, nor were the inspectors. Mycroft even refused to help. But we did it anyway. When we did, I took it to Mycroft first, expecting him to release it to a public clamoring for the name of the fiend and for closure. Imagine my shock when Mycroft threatened to have all of us tried for treason and killed. You see, it was the Queen's favourite doctor who was Jack the Ripper. Not the doctor-in-ordinary to the Queen, he was the official doctor, but her favourite one, Lord Carlton Blackwell."

At the mention of that name, Flora gasped. "Sherlock, that was Thomas's uncle! He was always touching me when he visited.

Pinning me in a cupboard and holding me by my neck. It was hard to stay out of his reach. He didn't often visit when I worked for the Blackwells because he often traveled with the Queen as she travelled. And he often went to the university to visit Thomas. I had no idea. I don't know what to say. I am at a loss for words."

Holmes reached for Flora's hand, kissed it, and continued. "We were all told by Mycroft, Mrs. Hudson included, that we were to sign confidentiality agreements stating we understood we would be tried for treason if we told anyone. We all signed because none of us wanted the others to suffer. However, we are all released from that contract now. So, now that we are caught up on that part. The next part is that the Blackwell name was given a change to Ledingford so the innocent members of the family would be protected in case anything ever came to light."

Holmes reached out to Flora and held her. "I'm so sorry, but it seems that every part of your life has been touched badly by this family. To be the one to tell you this, well, I'm learning that love can be painful sometimes." With that, Mrs. Hudson shook her head and laughed. "Oh, Sherlock! You will learn that love can indeed be painful sometimes. But the good always outweighs the bad." The tension melted from the room.

Chapter 27

A Dangerous Plan

"Go on, Sherlock. Now explain our plan." Flora said.

Holmes looked at Flora and Mrs. Hudson. I could tell from his look he had come up with a plan, and it was dangerous. I had seen that look many times before. He began, "Flora, I know I've just hit you with several shocks. If there was another way to make this happen and return your friend and the other women safely home, I would do it." Sherlock put his hand over Flora's again and gave it a loving squeeze. She smiled at him briefly in return. He continued, "But we need to move quickly. Too quickly, but we haven't a choice." He reached over to his end table and picked up a letter, and held it in his hand. The letter had been hand delivered to him while Flora and I were out.

"In this letter sent by messenger to me, Mycroft has informed me that the men responsible for the disappearance of the women have bought properties in three other counties. More women will go missing to be trafficked to these countries, and I'm sure women will be taken from those countries as well. This is a major criminal operation in the human sex trafficking of unfortunate and poor women, and as such, we have had Scotland Yard join forces with Mycroft's agents and the police and the proper government agencies of the three countries involved. We need to stop this here, where it began. We need to do it soon."

Mrs. Hudson came to sit with Flora and held her hand. Holmes moved back to his chair. I said, "Holmes, just tell us what we need to do. I can't imagine how these men came to the point of selling women for despicable sex acts. Depravity knows no bounds."

Holmes looked at me and said, "ah, Watson. Ever at the ready and always willing to step into the fray. I'm a sorry old man, but this is a woman's job. I wish that were not so. But time is of the essence. No matter how Mycroft, Lestrade, Gregson, and I tried to play this one out, it always came back to the women. Mrs. Hudson and Flora. But it is with much danger and risk on their part. I have spoken to our brave Mrs. Hudson earlier. I will ask my remarkable Flora to agree to our plans, the only workable plan, now."

"Holmes, you can't mean to tell me there is no other way except involving them. That can't be possible," I retorted.

"Watson, there are indeed other ways, but they would take time, and we do not have that. We also run the risk of this extensive group of men disappearing to these other countries and setting up shop anywhere. Then we never find the women at all, or we find them dead. We must get every man on the original two lists. Some may be innocent and will be given a heartfelt apology from Her Majesty's government. Those guilty will spend much time as a guest of Her Majesty's government...or worse. However, to do this, to play the chess game they are playing, we need them to capture our Queens. Mrs. Hudson and Flora."

"Holmes! Have you lost your mind!" I stood up and stared Holmes down.

"Doctor Watson. Please sit down." Flora looked at me with a strength I had seen before in my own dear wife as she lay dying. I sat.

"Sherlock, I think I see where you are going with this. I am the prize in Thomas's collection. He will want me back. If I'm taken, it will have to be with Mrs. Hudson as they know she will go right to you if she isn't taken too. You're betting on them not harming her because they haven't killed yet. You also know I would reinforce this by trading cooperation for not harming her. Thomas and the others would be excited with my capture, which would make them let their guard down and buy you time to coordinate your own operations to take everyone down at once. Am I correct?" Flora paused, still holding Mrs. Hudson's hand.

Holmes beamed at Flora with pride and much love in his eyes. Then his face turned to the seriousness befitting this situation. "That is exactly the plan. It would have to be tonight. Lord Ledingford will also be a guest at the dinner Mrs. Hudson is to attend, and Mycroft has arranged for you to be there as well. Flora, please know I cannot keep you safe once he takes you and Mrs.

Hudson from Brigadier Smith's home. Nor can I protect Mrs. Hudson. You will need to do that. And as I said to Mrs. Hudson, you can say no. Doing this will subject you to great harm. Thomas will indeed have you again."

Flora looked at him, shaking her head that she understood. "Sherlock, how long will you need to arrange things on your end?"

Holmes looked at her with a deep sadness, and he choked out his words. "Two days from today. Two days. Do you understand what that means?"

Flora looked him in the eye, unwavering in her braveness. "I do. It means he will, in all probability, drug me and rape me again. My love, I fully understand the risk. But we will be saving so many from the same fate. My dear friend Rose and the other women already being tortured by him and his friends will be freed. I have but one question. Are you sure we will get them all with this plan?"

The Keeper of the Flame

Ah, my Mary. You are so close I can smell you. You seem to enjoy going out with Doctor Watson. I've paid your waiter at the Criterion to tell me what the both of you are discussing. Trying to ruin my club, it seems. Well, we can't allow that. Tsk. Tsk. No matter. Once you are mine, you will become the star of my little club. Many men will pay to have you, my lovely moth.

You will be bedded by men and women from many countries, and I will become richer when you are on your back. But first, I will take you and break you once again. I'll watch the light go out of your eyes as you realize this is all there is for you. Remember Mary? It will be just like old times. It won't be long now.

I just need you to come out and play alone. Maybe I'll just kill this Watson and take you now. It's Holmes I want anyway. I want to see the look in his eyes as I'm taking you. As my friends take their turns with you. As he realizes he is helpless to save you. What do you think that would do to a man like him? Why I don't think he'd ever get out of the insane asylum, do you?

Holmes took something from me once. My uncle. My uncle's love. My father didn't love me at all. He barely tolerated me. But Uncle Jack understood my perversions. He encouraged them. He helped me refine them. He took you too that first time, back in that room in my father's house. He took you over and over and over for weeks. I'm truly sorry I had to kill him. Now I will finally take something from Sherlock Holmes... you, my Mary. You.

Chapter 28

A Proposal

"You are all crazy," I said to Holmes. I got up and walked to the window, and glared at the darkness outside. It matched the darkness I felt inside after hearing what I knew in my heart was the best plan and the only way with the time we had. Oh, but the cost! It was high. Too high. Holmes got up, and I watched his reflection in the window as he walked up behind me.

"Watson," he whispered. "Don't you know how this is tearing my heart from my body? I'm going to ask Flora to marry me, to be my wife, but I am also sending her into the lion's den. But Watson, I cannot let this man continue. Flora understands the risks here. I myself understand them all too well. The two women I love best in the world are braver than I could ever hope to be. Do you know why?" I shook my head no. "Because they will be helping others of their sex. Women are a true sisterhood. They are much better than the brotherhood of man. They pull together when helping each other. It doesn't matter if they know each other or even like each other. When one needs help, they close ranks. And the less they have, the more they help. Women are truly remarkable. Come, Watson. Time is wasting. We must plan."

Reluctantly, Holmes led me to my chair. Mrs. Hudson had

moved to Holmes' chair, and Holmes sat on the sofa with Flora. Holmes directed his next words to Flora and Mrs. Hudson, "Doctor Watson is angered by the fact we want both of you to do something so filled with danger, and I think he's feeling a bit of anger toward the both of you as well. I know he is angry with me. Let's discuss this now, and then it needs to be done. We cannot go into this plan with other things on our minds. The potential for failure would be too great. Failure here means the both of you could be seriously hurt or die. I shall begin."

Holmes continued, "Flora, I must say that Watson knew I loved you before I did. It's the one time he not only observed, but he saw." I gave a chuckle to Holmes at that but then went stone-faced again, and Holmes went on. "I thought I was in love with Irene Adler, 'the' woman. But next to you, she pales in comparison. You are so much like me that you are a part of me. Where you begin and I end, I don't know. So, when I tell you that asking you to do this will most certainly allow for that monster to violate you, I want to run. I want to take you and run far from here. But I would have every woman that's hurt or killed by these men on my conscience for the rest of my life. There is nowhere I could run to get away from that. I only hope that you can find it in your heart to forgive me for directly causing you to go through the very pain I want to protect you from."

Holmes then turned to face Mrs. Hudson. "My interminable

Mrs. Hudson. You have been as a mother to me. Though all believe we met because of these rooms for rent at 221b, we go back much farther than that." I registered my shock to Holmes at that last statement, but I did not interrupt. "I would not be here if it wasn't for you, but that is another story. I am literally risking your very life, asking you to continue with this plan, and that breaks my heart. But if I forbade you to do it, would that matter? I think not."

Mrs. Hudson looked at Holmes with a smile in her eyes. "Oh, Sherlock, you could never forbid me to do anything that was in my mind and heart to do. Flora knows what to say to ensure my life, and if they try a slap and tickle, well, I'm older, and it might be my last chance." Holmes and Flora stopped stock still and then began laughing. They laughed so hard that they doubled over, as did Mrs. Hudson. I looked at them with such anger. How dare they disrespect the depth of the danger they were in with this show of laughter. Then a light dawned on me. It wasn't disrespecting the danger; it was a deep respect for it. They understood it completely and refused to let it take their humanity. I looked at them with new respect and deep love. I began to laugh too!

After we calmed ourselves, Flora spoke next. "Sherlock, I think I loved you before I met you. You had certainly won my mind with your tracts and monographs. Now you have my heart. What we will be doing will prevent many from suffering. That's a very noble cause indeed. What we are doing now, right here, is something that the ladies of Whitechapel did when they went out to face the dangers they faced every night. I did it too. We talked before we went out to sell our bodies. We met in odd places, like under the pale yellow street lamp, and reassured each other that we had no choice in what we were doing; we did it to live. We knew that if we lived through that night, we would love and respect each other the next morning. We had a bond that allowed us to face the danger of the evening and survive. We will all survive this too. Intact. With love. Intact. With respect. It is our bond."

I got to speak last, and it was good that I did. I was looking at this from how could they, but it's actually how could they not. I saw that now. "First, let me apologize for earlier. You have all made me understand this plan much better. It must be done as dangerous as it is. I will do that which I need to do to keep you all safe and to patch you up if it comes to that. I love each one of you, and together, we will do this no matter how hard, no matter the risk." I could go on no further as I was beginning to get choked up. So, I cleared my throat and waited for Holmes to speak again.

Holmes rescued me when he saw I could speak no further. "Well, though we have much planning to do, the good inspectors and my brother Mycroft will not be here for a few minutes yet. I was not going to do this until this case was done. I certainly was not going to do this publicly, but I can think of no better time than now, after our heartfelt conversations. Holmes turned to Flora and kissed her cheek. He stood, straightened his jacket, got down on one knee, and said, "my brave, loving, and wonderful Flora. You hold my heart in your hands, crush it, and I will die, but embrace it, and you would bring me all the joy a man could possibly hope for." He reached into his pocket and pulled out a small box. "Flora James, will you do me the greatest honour of my life and marry me?" You could hear a pin drop in the room. Everyone was quiet. Flora was staring in shock. She looked at Holmes and then hugged him tightly. We heard her say yes. She repeated it over and over and over until Holmes took the ring from the box, slipped the ring on her finger, and silenced her with a kiss so passionate that it left both Mrs. Hudson and me blushing to our ears.

"Holmes, old man. Please let me be the first to congratulate you both." I shook his hand and embraced him, and kissed Flora's cheeks. I turned and went to the kitchen to get a bottle of champagne and some glasses. Mrs. Hudson held them both in her arms softly crying tears of joy. She was still doing so when I came back with the champagne. I poured a glass for everyone as Billy opened the door, followed by Mycroft and the inspectors. The confused expressions on their faces made us double over with laughter once again.

Chapter 29

The Toast

Mycroft looked at Holmes, and a split second later, he said, "well, Sherlock, brother mine, I expect congratulations are in order."

Lestrade said, "Someone, please tell me what's going on. I thought we were here for some very serious plans, and I do not see that reflected on your faces or in the demeanour of the room."

Mrs. Hudson said, "gentlemen, Sherlock just proposed to Flora, and she said yes. We were just about to pour a champagne toast. Would you care to toast the happy couple before we must plan for what certainly will be a few days of the utmost danger?"

Lestrade looked a bit sheepish after Mrs. Hudson's dressing down. But he went directly over to Holmes and Flora for hearty good wishes. Gregson joined him, and Mrs. Hudson went for more glasses as I poured champagne. Even Billy was allowed a small glass.

Mycroft waited until the inspectors had given him the room he needed to get to the couple. He kissed Flora's cheeks and shook Holmes' hand. I passed the champagne around, and we held our glasses and waited for the toasts to begin.

Billy was first because his enthusiasm at being allowed a short tot of champagne burst through propriety. "Mr. Holmes, Miss Flora, I'm happy for ya and happier for the fizz." He held his glass up proudly, and I reminded him we do not drink until all the toasts are finished. He pulled his arm down and looked so downcast as he stared at his bit of fizz that we all smiled at him in sympathy.

Gregson took his turn. "Mr. Holmes, Flora, I wish you both much happiness. I can see you have much love. I hope both continue for many years to come."

Lestrade stepped forward. "Sherlock, Flora, I can't say I'm surprised after seeing the both of you working together of late. But I can say I never thought I'd see the day that Sherlock would find someone that took him out of himself long enough to fall in love. Cheers to both of you."

I spoke next. "Holmes, it has been an adventure since the first day we met. I must say this adventure was unexpected but certainly not unwelcome. I've watched how Flora has changed you. I noticed it that first night at the lecture, though you would not admit it then. This upcoming marriage is a good thing. And I'm honoured to have heard your proposal, though it made me cry like a baby."

Mrs. Hudson stood before Holmes and Flora. Her hanky already in her hand. "Sherlock, my dear boy, you have always had an air of luck about you. But meeting Flora has been the best luck you've had. Flora, your life has been less fortunate, but you have all of us now. You knew Sherlock came with a funny and odd little family, but you said yes anyway. That means you are already our family." She dabbed her eyes as she turned to look at Mycroft as he cleared his throat to speak.

"Sherlock, brother mine, I could not be prouder of you now than I was when you solved the myriad of cases for the Queen and her government. I have always told you I was the more intelligent brother. Today you proved that untrue. Only someone with true intelligence would understand what a gem they had in Miss James; uhm, I think I should call you Flora now as you will be a welcome sister-in-law."

We all turned to the couple, cheered, and drank our toast. Billy punctuated our glasses being placed back on the tray by saying, "thank goodness that's over. I was parched!"

Mrs. Hudson suddenly yelled STOP! All of us were frozen on the spot. She said, "I've just realized I haven't seen this ring yet, Flora. Give her here." Flora presented her hand to Mrs. Hudson, who took it and admired a beautiful and rare navy blue moonstone encircled by beautifully cut pink diamonds, Flora's favourite colours. Mrs. Hudson said that Sherlock had outdone himself, and we were free to resume what we were doing now. Everyone not clearing up glasses found seats and braced for what was to come.

Chapter 30

Not an Unfortunate

Mrs. Hudson and I cleared the glasses and champagne bottle, and Billy turned the chalkboards and made sure fresh chalk was put out in case of need. We all took seats, with Mycroft remaining standing and Holmes and Lestrade were in chairs close by. Billy sat in the barrel chair, his favourite seat. Mrs. Hudson and Flora sat together on the sofa. We were ready to draw up our plans to stop this awful trafficking club once and for all.

As we began, there was knocking on the downstairs door. Billy ran down and opened the outer door. We soon heard him coming back up with another set of footsteps. It was a constable. He motioned for Lestrade. The two of them retreated into the hallway, and we could hear muffled voices, then footsteps down the stairs and the front door closing. Lestrade came back in, head down. He held the back of a chair for support and sighed as he looked up at us. "Another woman was taken. It was not unfortunate this time. It seems that the owner of the Whitechapel bookshop's wife was taken ill. He sent his sixteen-year-old daughter to the chemist for medicine. She never returned. Her reticule was found near the alley. By now, you know which alley. The one under the pale yellow street lamp. So, we have seven women taken now. My constable also reported that he looked back in the logs, and there were several more reports of women missing but with not enough information to investigate.

There was a hush in the room. No one spoke. No one moved. Holmes broke the silence. "Please, I suggest we begin. Flora and Mrs. Hudson need to get ready to attend the dinner with Mycroft at Brigadier Charles Smith's later tonight. We cannot afford the luxury of time to think about this any further."

Mycroft, still standing, spoke, "for any not understanding the plan, here it is. Tonight, we will be placing both Mrs. Hudson and Flora in a most dangerous situation indeed. Lord Ledingford will be at the dinner this evening, and we will be allowing, no, making it easy, for him to abduct Flora, but not without having to take Mrs. Hudson with her. The reason for this is so there is not an immediate absconding with Flora to someplace else. He will need to plan more carefully for having two high-profile women in his custody. It will be entirely up to Flora to keep Mrs. Hudson alive by acquiescing to Ledingford's demands only if no harm comes to Mrs. Hudson. You will see this creates a danger to Flora already. Her personal safety. She will be trading her body for Mrs. Hudson's very life."

He continued, "Ledingford is a braggart. He will plan a showing of his prize. The inside information I have is that they are entertaining guests from the three countries where they are in the process of opening clubs. That will happen two days from tomorrow night at Ledingford's home, where the club meets. He will definitely want to show off his prize that day. That day is when we move in and arrest them. We will hopefully have enough people in place to do that and ensure the safety of the women also held at Ledingford's home at the same time. We cannot take any chances, nor can there be one mistake. Again, from tonight until two days hence, Flora will ensure the safety of Mrs. Hudson but is doing that at a very high cost to her person."

The room was deathly quiet. The crackle of the fire was the only sound. Holmes spoke. "Flora, I would be doing a disservice to my future wife if I didn't say to you that you can change your mind. We can try and find another way."

Flora looked around the room, then to Holmes. "No. This is the best way. If we can arrest those from the other countries too, then we have a better chance of stopping the trafficking of women altogether. I know I'll be his prize trophy, and though I know I will, in all probability, be brutally used by him again, I may be able to learn much that we can use against him after they are all arrested. Mrs. Hudson will be safe with me, I assure you. Thomas would rather take my body if I were cooperative. He'll threaten Mrs. Hudson, and I will agree to what he wants. He'll think he is in control. Just assure us that in two days you will come. Please."

Mycroft and Lestrade both spoke up. They assured her that

no matter if everything was in place or not that they would come in for them no later than those two days. Mycroft said the officials from the other countries were on their way, and two days hence were the earliest they would arrive. They demanded to be present at the arrest as their countries' citizens would be arrested too. The diplomacy between the three countries and the United Kingdom was at stake. However, Mycroft said at the end of the two days, diplomacy be damned. Lestrade said that help from not only the Metropolitan Police but from police outside of London would also be in place then.

Then Holmes spoke. "Mycroft has been planning with me to try and arrange to get me, as a potential interest from yet another country, into the party the club is having. While that does not protect Flora and Mrs. Hudson from tonight until the event two nights hence, it will help to have someone inside to help them and the other seven women get to safety when Lestrade's and Mycroft's people invade the home."

Mycroft spoke to everyone then. "I will be heading back to the Diogenes Club to ready myself for this evening. Lestrade's men and Sherlock's irregulars, headed by Billy here, will be stationed outside the Brigadier's home to be sure that the ladies are unharmed when taken and that they are indeed taken to Ledingford's home and not someplace else. I bid you all good evening."

Mycroft made his way out of the flat and down the stairs to his private hansom. Then Billy begged everyone to excuse him to get the irregulars ready. Holmes gave him a small sack of coins and Mrs. Hudson gave him a large hamper of food and drink to take with him to share with those on the job with him this evening. Billy took his leave.

Lestrade said, "I need to be leaving with Gregson here to oversee our watch tonight. We have police stationed from the Brigadiers to Ledingfords. We will know if they try to deviate, and we will get Mrs. Hudson and Flora away from them if that happens. If they are taken to Ledingford's, we have teams stationed there with changes every four hours to keep them fresh and on their toes. As soon as the police from the other countries arrive, we will coordinate with Mycroft and the government officials he's waiting for to make a simultaneous bust-in with rescuing the ladies and making all arrests." Lestrade and Gregson said their goodbyes and took their leave.

Watson walked downstairs with Mrs. Hudson. She had told Flora to come downstairs when she was ready to dress for dinner. Suddenly Sherlock and Flora found themselves alone in the room.

Chapter 31

Sherlock and Flora

I went to Flora and enfolded her with my arms. We stood that way for a while, letting the calmness and the crackle of the fireplace wash over us. We were drawing strength from each other as well. Both of us were strong-willed and strong-minded. But this case had pulled at us, trying to weaken our strength and, by that, our love. We would not allow that to happen.

Flora looked up into my eyes and I kissed her. I could feel her melt into me. Soft. Vulnerable. Loving. Maybe Watson was correct. Maybe we were all mad. Flora held me tighter and whispered her love. I found strength in that. I found strength in her. I held her out at arm's length and looked into her eyes. "Ready?" I spoke. "Yes, my love," she said. "I'm ready now. I'd like to finish this. I've a wedding to plan, you know!" I laughed. "Ah, my Flora. Ever practical. Be off with you then. Mrs. Hudson awaits. Please send Watson back upstairs." "Of course," Flora said. And with a kiss on my cheek, Flora ran down the stairs.

Chapter 32

Preparations

"Mrs. Hudson, are you afraid?" Flora asked as the Queen bees of this night were dressing.

"Oh yes. Sherlock told me when you aren't afraid, you make mistakes. Of course, one could be too afraid, I suppose. But I'm not. I just must look pretty and act as a damsel in distress. You, my sweet Flora, have the rocky part. Do you think you can stop him from having his way with you?"

Flora thought for a moment. "No. No, I don't. He will take me as he has before. But I will be drugged. I can only hope I don't remember what he does to me. I don't remember all of what he did in the past, but it was months after he sold me to that brothel that I could walk, or even move, without pain."

"Oh, Flora," said Mrs. Hudson. Let me ask you one last time. Is this what you really want?

Flora stopped putting her rouge powder on and looked at Mrs. Hudson. "It is. It would tear me apart knowing I could have helped but did not. It's the right thing to do. Now come on. Up we march for the inspection of the troops by commanders Watson and Holmes."

Holmes and Watson were sitting in their chairs, Watson with

his cigar and Holmes with his pipe, planning how to approach the home of Ledingford a few nights hence when the rescue would begin. They had heard the ladies come up the ſtairs, but they were engrossed in what they were doing and didn't ſtop until the ladies were ſtanding next to them.

Flora tapped Holmes' shoulder as I looked up at her too. "Do we look all right? We muſt leave shortly. Holmes had begun to say in a minute, but he didn't get very far getting the words out. Flora was a vision in a robin's egg blue silk gown with silver threads running through it that glinted in the light from the fireplace and she looked every part of the goddess. Her hair, thanks to Mrs. Hudson, was up in soft curls with a silver and navy blue moonſtone tiara weaved within the curls. Ravishing was the word. Flora was ravishing. Holmes took her hand and spun her around. "You'll do," he said. "Really, Holmes, I said. "Your fiancé is a goddess."

Everyone turned to Mrs. Hudson and admired how she played up the governess angle. It was quite brilliant, really. She looked ſtately and regal in a muted navy gown. Her hair was pulled back and up but framed by the shimmering gold tiara. Underſtated. It would be difficult to speak to her in any way other than respectfully. She could handle her charge and she would demand nothing but respect.

"Well, it would seem you both need no more coaching from

Watson or me. You are remarkable women and this country, and my brother, will owe you both a debt they cannot possibly pay. With that, Billy, who had returned to pick up more food supplies, came running up the steps to tell the ladies Mycroft was there for them.

Billy entered the room and he literally skidded to a stop and gasped at Flora and Mrs. Hudson. "Cor, and gawd lord almighty, you ladies are beautiful tonight." The ladies thanked Billy and asked him to accompany them downstairs. But first, Flora went to Sherlock. "I think a Christmas wedding will do. Just a few friends and family. Then maybe a honeymoon to Brighton. Don't you think so? Sherlock said, "I heartily agree. It is close, but after looking at you and Mrs. Hudson this evening, I believe that both of you can perform miracles. " Flora kissed him lightly on the lips and turned to catch up with Mrs. Hudson and Billy on the steps. He wanted, as the woman he was going to marry left a place of safety knowing she would be badly hurt, for her to hold something good in her heart. He felt his own heart would burst with respect and love for her, but also fear for her on this night.

Chapter 33

Into the Lion's Den

The driver of Mycroft's gleaming black coach stepped down and handed the ladies inside to Mycroft, who greeted them warmly. His respect for these two women knew no bounds, and he understood his brother's love and devotion to them. Billy attached himself to the back of the coach for an easy drop-off at a place where the driver agreed to slow down so Billy could meet up with the irregulars scheduled for first watch. The driver climbed back atop his perch and waited a few moments for the ladies to become comfortable, then headed the coach to Brigadier Charles Smith's home.

Mycroft spoke to the ladies. "Mrs. Hudson, Flora, please know that any time before we reach the Brigadier's home, you can still change your mind. No one, least of all myself, will think any less of you if you choose not to do this. This is a dangerous game we are playing, and the only chess pieces we have are our Queens. I know that most men would cower if asked to do what each of you are being asked to do for the next few nights. Men who are trained to take risks." He paused to give Mrs. Hudson and Flora a chance to speak.

Flora deferred to Mrs. Hudson and let her speak first. "Mycroft, you know my history with your brother. Sherlock is the bravest man I know, but something as small as a few powdered specks nearly killed him. These men are those powdered specks to these women, but they are much larger specks. What chance do you think they have? They will be used over and over. Abused and hurt, they will die young and be replaced by other women these fiends abduct. How can I, a woman too, let that happen just by saying I'm afraid and then go on with my life? My safe life. I cannot. I will, I want, to do this, Mycroft."

Flora squeezed Mrs. Hudson's hand and began addressing Mycroft herself. "I was repeatedly raped by Thomas and his friends, day and night, over and over, violated in every way a woman can be. Brutally. I know, I personally know, what these women are feeling. The pain and anguish they are suffering. The abandonment by their fellow man. The abandonment by their fellow women. Knowing this, I cannot shrink from my duty of helping them. Mycroft, I will do this no matter what happens to my body. It's my mind I will keep. I will see those poor women taken from Thomas and the lot of those men imprisoned. I can do no less."

Mycroft looked at these brave women again and realized that his brother was lucky indeed to have both in his life. The coach was now approaching the Brigadier's home. The driver slowed briefly and Billy dropped silently from the coach into the streets to find his friends. The game was on!

Chapter 34

A Reunion of Sorts

Mycroft exited the coach with much help from the driver, then he turned and extended his hand to Mrs. Hudson and me in turn. There were two butlers at the huge double doors leading into the foyer of the Brigadier's stately home. They pulled the doors open together as we approached. We walked into a foyer that was enormous. The floor tiles were black and white, and the huge chandelier glowed with what seemed like hundreds of candles that made the floor sparkle. Because we were with Mycroft, we were ushered right in, and a valet and maid began taking our wraps. There was a magnificent round table in the centre of the room. It was filled with the most beautiful displays of hothouse flowers in every colour. Two curved staircases circled the outside of the room and led up to a mezzanine where flags of the British Empire hung from the balustrade. There was an archway past the side of the table which led into a huge ballroom. It was there Mycroft was leading us. My heart was beating faster. This was it. No turning back now. The game is certainly afoot!

"Mycroft!" A gentleman called from one of the tables encircling the outside of the room. He stood and walked over to meet us. "Mycroft, please introduce me to the lovely women you have

122

brought to my little dinner." Little dinner, I thought. He's not showing off for his boss now, is he? I put my hand atop Mycroft's as he held it up for me. Mrs. Hudson walked beside us. "Ah, Charles. Please let me introduce you to my brother Sherlock's intended. Miss Flora James and her guardian for the evening Mrs. Hudson. Mrs. Hudson approached him first, extending her hand. He kissed it and said, "charmed." Then Flora approached, and he kissed both cheeks lingering much too long than what was proper. Mycroft looked the other way. I said, "Brigadier Smith, your home is lovely." He replied, "Please call me Charles." The game had begun. He knows who I am.

Mycroft turned to us and said, "Ladies, there are some men I need to see. Please take a walk around the room, I should be back by then and we shall attend the dinner together." The Brigadier said he'd walk with us and that there was someone he wanted us to meet, but they had not yet arrived. No wondering about who that might be. He extended his hand out to me and Mrs. Hudson slipped right in and took it instead. Then she positively beamed as she smiled at him. He wrapped her hand under his arm, and we began to walk. I was aware of Mycroft in the doorway. He was engaged in conversation with two other men, but he was following us with his eyes. As we walked around the room, the Brigadier introduced us to many men and women. Lords, Ladies, barristers, military men, businessmen, government men, and Dukes, especially that young one one causing so much trouble for his brother, his father, and his grandmother, Her Majesty the Queen. I was unimpressed. He was really nothing much at all. As we were halfway around the room, the garden doors opened and standing there with a predatory smile was Thomas. I shuddered involuntarily.

"Thomas, do come in," said the Brigadier. "There is someone I want you to meet. "

"Well, Charles, look what we have here. Mary Kelly back from the dead. Or rather Flora now. No matter, still my moth. And who is this? Why I do believe it's Mrs. Hudson, the landlady of Sherlock Holmes, Consulting Detective. A chaperone, my dear? Really, don't you think it's way too late for that? I know every orifice of your body most intimately already." He stepped forward and put his arm around my waist and pulled me flat against his body. I could see Mrs. Hudson try to release her arm from Charles', but he was holding her arm tightly.

Thomas held me tightly against his body as he moved me outside the door to the garden and backed me into a tree. He pulled my skirts up and reached inside my undergarments and grabbed me intimately. Thomas began kissing me and moving his body against me. I couldn't breathe. I flashed back to the first time he had taken me and I tried to push him away. He had me pinned. Suddenly Mycroft was at the door. "Really, Thomas, it's before dinner and you are already beginning the pudding. Come inside with my brother's intended, and at least wait until we've all had our dinner." He reached his hand out toward me and beckoned me to come to him. Only then did Thomas release me.

He looked at Mycroft and said, "Tell me, Mycroft, does your brother know how many men have had this whore? Oh, of course he does. He's a consulting detective. I only hope he uses her like she's used to. It would be a shame not to give her what she likes." Thomas then brushed roughly past Mycroft, Charles, and Mrs. Hudson, who now had her arm free, and he entered the ballroom.

"My dear, are you alright?" Asked Mycroft. I said, "yes, but he is even more vile than I remembered. He couldn't wait to humiliate me."

I turned to look at Mrs. Hudson. "Are you all right? I saw Charles holding you tightly so that you couldn't come to my aid. Did he hurt you?"

"No, he didn't hurt me, but he angered me mightily. I saw Thomas take you out into the garden and begin accosting you, and Charles would not release my arm so I could go to you. He made me stay here and watch." Mrs. Hudson said.

"Well, at least we know that everyone in this room who is part of his little club knows who we are, so abducting us will be easier than Sherlock and I thought. No one will aid us, and Mycroft will make his leave after dinner and ask Charles to see us home after dancing. I expect we will be here until those with wives accompanying them have gone." I adjusted my gown a bit and stared across the room where Thomas and a few other men were talking. One of them looked at me. He began rubbing the front of his pants and licked his lips. I recognized him. It was Thomas's best friend, William. I turned away, repulsed.

Mycroft, at the sound of chimes, took both of our hands and wrapped them over his arms. "Ladies, dinner is served. This way. Do please try to eat as much as you can. I don't know how much food either of you will get after tonight." We walked again under the arch and to the left at the flowered table in the foyer to a magnificent dining room with a servant behind every chair of the longest dining table I'd ever seen. I looked at Mrs. Hudson, and she smiled at me. She is indeed a brave woman, into what felt like our last meal, we walked.

The Keeper of the Flame

Oh, bliss! Oh, wonder! Oh Finally! Moth, you are here. Mine again. I shall never let you go. I will have to punish you, of course. A brutally delectable punishment and if you live through it, you will be my moth, my whore, and I shall let the most brutal men in society use you as they like...for a price, a high price. I shall feed you my new drug and you will beg men to take you. Shall I put you on a leash and parade you around at my gatherings, ready to service men and women, as I say and as they pay, of course! I think that sounds lovely, don't you, my moth?

But first, your punishment. I will take you tonight, here, on the floor, like the whore you are. I'm sure watching it will excite my guests and they may take you after I'm finished with you. Many have already paid for the privilege in advance, but all after your punishment, of course. I will enjoy beating you as I have Mrs. Hudson held to watch. Do you know I have sold her to our Russian market? The soldier's pet until they kill her, they will use her well and teach her new ways of pleasing them. Age doesn't matter to them. She fetched a pretty price, Sherlock Holmes' landlady.

I saw you arrive thinking once again above your station on the arm of the elder Holmes. You looked lovely in your gown, but you shall never wear another after tonight. Never wear any clothes. A moth does not wear clothes. Ah, the chimes, dinner is served. You are to be the pudding. The taste of you in the garden after I licked my fingers made me hunger and I had to absent myself for a moment to take your friend Rose while I thought of you. I brought her here to service the help. They give us better service that way. Now I will finally take you, so eat well, my moth, my whore. You will need all your strength for my boots and my fists, and my cock. Isn't punishment divine?

Chapter 35

Dinner is Served

Mycroft, Mrs. Hudson, and I were seated directly across from Thomas. The pre-dinner conversation was muted and reserved. I talked easily with Mycroft and Mrs. Hudson. I learned more about Sherlock. What a funny little boy he must have been. Mycroft said he would want to investigate everything and take things apart to see how they worked. He wasn't, however, keen on how they went back together. It was just knowing how it was made, then he was done. He told a story of how Sherlock had built a bomb in his bedroom one day to show off to some friends. He told his mother he was building it, but she somehow didn't believe him and went about her household business. Suddenly there was a loud bang and little Sherlock came running down the stairs, preceded by his friends, who promptly ran out the front door. "What happened then?" I asked Mycroft.

"Then, our mother looked at him and said, 'why Sherlock, why do you do these things?' and he replied, 'why to see if I can mother, of course', at which time our mother just sat on the sofa and shook her head!"

"Oh, Mycroft," I said, "I would have loved to see that little boy. He's so serious and studious now. But he still does take things apart to see if he can." Mycroft shook his head yes to that. He smiled when he talked about young Sherlock. I felt the love the brothers had despite their seemingly tenuous relationship now.

Mrs. Hudson said, "oh yes, he does do that. Why imagine how I felt cleaning his flat and finding a human head in an ice chest? Or looking in a cup of tea and seeing something staring back at me. Sherlock still does things to see if he can, but he leaves them around for others to find!"

Conversation waned and the meal service began. It was military in its precision. Each servant came to a stop behind the person being served. Then, when all were in place, every one of them served the course at the same time. If we were here for any other reason, I would have loved this. But I looked at Mycroft and Mrs. Hudson beside him, and all I could manage was a weak smile.

The food was not only served impeccably but it was also plated exquisitely and it was delicious. The first course was Soup a la Reine, which glistened under the candlelight. It was served with a sherry beside it. The second course was oysters on the shell with a dry Chablis. The third course was sole with Newburg sauce and a Sauvignon Blanc. The fourth course was Beef Collops au Bordelaise with a lovely Claret. The fifth course was a green salad with mayonnaise dressing and stilton, bleu, and sharp cheddar cheese with fruits. The final course was a luscious rum-soaked trifle and a flaming figgy pudding brought out with fanfare and plenty of champagne. Mrs. Hudson and I tried both. So did Mycroft. We were then served coffee demitasse, which is very strong, so it was served with chocolates on the side. I thought I would have a hard time eating, but I did not. I finished course after course. I could see Mrs. Hudson enjoying her food too. And Mycroft, well, he was a man who always enjoyed the food.

As the meal was winding down, I stole a look at Thomas. William was standing behind him and they were speaking. Both were watching me. Feeling happy and full at this moment, I smiled and looked away. But I knew what would be coming next.

As if on cue, Mycroft said, "ladies, I will be speaking my regrets to our host and leaving now. I will ask if Charles could see to your arriving home safely because both of you want to stay for the after-dinner music and dance. He will most heartily agree and will most likely come to escort both of you back into the ballroom. After that, it's up to you."

Both of us thanked him and told him we would see him in two more nights. We all stood and Mycroft beckoned Charles to come over. "Charles, old man, the ladies want to stay for the dancing. I, however, do not. Would you see your coach takes them home when they are ready!"

"Mycroft, of course. We will enjoy having them to dance with. So very few women stay. And I will try to get them home at a decent hour. I hope everything was to your liking.". Mycroft said everything was splendid and thanked him profusely for agreeing to take us home.

Mrs. Hudson and I thanked Mycroft for a lovely evening, and he kissed our cheeks and went for his coat and then the door. While Mycroft was getting his coat, hands grabbed Mrs. Hudson and me and we were pulled up the stairs to the mezzanine. One on each side. Thomas was behind me, William behind Mrs. Hudson. When Mycroft was in his coat and hat, Thomas yelled at him. Once he found where the voice was coming from and looked up, Thomas bent me over the balustrade, held me down by my neck, and began making lewd movements behind me. I was hanging on to the flags trying not to fall over. He yelled to Mycroft, "tell Sherlock I had her first, I will have her now, and I'll have her always. Oh, and if she doesn't cooperate," with that … " Across the balustrade William held a knife to Mrs. Hudson's throat. He pushed her head over the balustrade and held her there. Thomas continued, "If my moth doesn't cooperate, Mrs. Hudson's throat will be slit, and she will be pushed over a balustrade somewhere in London without the benefit of clothes or distinguishing items. She will be buried in an unmarked pauper's grave as just another dead whore." Then Mycroft was forcibly ejected from the Brigadier's house.

Chapter 36
Mycroft Visits 221b

Mycroft's hansom pulled up to 221b and having had been at the window, I ran down to let him in. We exchanged no words as we trudged back up the 17 steps in complete silence. Mycroft was as pale as a sheet and shaking like a leaf. He sat in my chair and stared at the floor. I poured him a brandy and placed the glass in his hand and then sat in the barrel chair to wait.

I watched Mycroft stare at Holmes for a second and look back down, and I put my head down as Mycroft had done. When the Holmes boys were excited, worried, angry, or any of a spate of emotions most humans would find normal, they became broodingly silent. So now we wait, I thought. I began tapping the side of the barrel chair out of nervousness. Holmes, younger, turned and looked at me. "Watson, perhaps you would be happier waiting in your bedroom rather than sitting here quietly with the rest of the adults." I placed my hands in my lap silently. And we continued to wait.

After 15 minutes, Mycroft raised the brandy snifter to his lips and drained the glass in one gulp. He looked at Holmes and said, "I fear we have made a big mistake." He explained what the evening was like in detail. It was upsetting but no more that we had anticipated. That was until he told us about his leaving. "Sherlock, if you could only have seen the madness in his eyes. I thought he might be inappropriate with Flora. In my mind, I thought it. Intellectually. But when I saw him with his hand in her undergarments and then bending her over and holding her neck and making those obscene movements, I knew she hadn't a chance of fending him off. He will rape her. And when William, so calm and casual, held that knife to Mrs. Hudson's throat and made to push her from the balustrade, I thought I was the one dying. The way they casually said if Flora didn't cooperate in every demand, then they would slit Mrs. Hudson's throat and push her naked, with nothing to identify who she is, over a balustrade somewhere in London, I thought I would die on the spot. Right there. In the foyer. We, I, underestimated them. Sherlock, this is very bad indeed."

Holmes thought for a moment and jumped up from his chair and went to the window. After a moment, he turned back to face us. "There is no way to change the plan now. We go with everything we planned and get them out. Flora will keep Mrs. Hudson safe. The cost will be to her. To my Flora. My love. My heart. My soul. We knew that. She and I knew that. We talked long into the afternoon about it. The only question she had for me was, will I still love her after this beast takes her again? My answer was there would be no reason not to love her when she was knowingly putting herself in harm's way to save friends and strangers after learning what it would cost her. As her future husband, I feel I've let her down, but she assured me that was not true. And it isn't true that any of you have let her down, either. So, for her sake and safety and that of Mrs. Hudson, we stick to the plan and prepare our rescue and arrests."

Holmes looked at them and said, "Tonight, Lestrade, Gregson, and the irregulars will assure Flora and Mrs. Hudson get to Ledingford's home and nowhere else. Tomorrow, they will meet us here and we will continue to plan. The following day, we meet again and get into our places and do this and do it well where all the women are rescued and the men responsible arrested. Mycroft, you need to arrange with your people who from the foreign countries' representatives are coming with us to the arrests. Be sure all of them are well vetted because we want no surprises. Mycroft, if you are well enough to leave, please begin now. Watson and I will study the plans of the house as Lestrade and Gregson will study their copy. They will plan the best access to trap them inside and dispatch officers to apprehend them before harm can come to the women. Watson and I will plan how he and the irregulars will follow the police in and get the women to waiting police wagons to get to the hospital for medical help. And Mycroft, get me into that soirée they are planning because that is where I'll be."

With that, Mycroft rose from my chair, and I accompanied him down the stairs. When I returned to Holmes, he had the knife that was in Flora's side in his hands. He looked at me with fire in his usually cool grey eyes and said, "Watson, I do believe I will enjoy returning this knife to Ledingford."

Chapter 37

The Rape

Flora held Mrs. Hudson's hand in the ballroom of the Brigadier's home. The music was still playing by quite talented musicians, but she and Mrs. Hudson were the only two women there. No one danced. It felt ominous. Dark. An eerie calm before the storm. The candles had burned low, many flickered out. The men who were left in the ballroom circled them like spiders encircling their webbed prey. Flora knew many of them. She was raped by some and had serviced others during her time in the brothel, but never a time when she walked the streets on her own. She would never bed these men again. Willingly.

Flora spoke to them, "Are there none here who are real men? Are there none who can see this is wrong? Are you all blinded by sex and money? Will none of you help us?"

Thomas parted the throng of men, well more than the 43 who were left on the lists and stood in front of Flora. He raised his hand high and slapped her so hard she fell to the floor. Two men grabbed Mrs. Hudson so she could not assist Flora in what was to come. Then Thomas kicked her repeatedly. Over and over. He was screaming, "you are my moth. I will never let you forget that. I will abuse you so badly no man would ever want you again, not even your precious Sherlock." Flora curled into a ball with her arms over her head. A

136

hand grabbed her arm and wrenched her up so fast she lost her bearings. More hands held her as Thomas began beating Flora in the stomach with his fists. After her head sank down, he began cutting off her gown and undergarments. He grabbed the back of her hair and pulled her face up. He screamed into her face, "moths do not get to wear clothes, ever!" He released her hair and continued speaking, "tonight, you will be used by me and right here on the ballroom floor like the whore you are. You will not be drugged this time. I want you to remember every degrading second. I want you to feel every pain that will most definitely be inflicted on you. Mrs. Hudson here can watch, so in case you forget or pass out, she can remind you. My club members will watch them they will take you. You will be dehumanized and degraded. You need to learn your place."

With that horrific statement, Mrs. Hudson was pulled into a chair and tied down opposite the circle of men, trying to get closer to see this upstart moth learn her lesson. He looked at Mrs. Hudson as men stood next to her and behind her watching Thomas and said, "I hope this brings back memories of the beating and rapes you suffered at your husband's hands. It's why you could never bear children, isn't it?" Mrs. Hudson shrank back and stared at Thomas. "Yes, I do my research too." Men began rubbing Mrs. Hudson's shoulders and reaching into her bodice, grabbing her breasts as Thomas began to disrobe. As he stood there naked, he said to the men, "well, let the floor show begin." The music reached a crescendo and then stopped. The musicians came to watch as well get their turn. The men holding Flora threw her to the floor as Thomas mounted her, choking her neck with both his hands as Flora's legs kicked at the floor.

Mrs. Hudson screamed.

Chapter 38

What Billy and Gregson Saw

Lestrade, Gregson, the irregulars, and the police who were assigned to the few different routes from the Brigadier's to Lord Ledingford's home were on their guard now. The early word was that several or more coaches were lined up in front of the Brigadier's house and all were ready to move.

Billy was closest to the house when he saw rough hands practically dragging a bedraggled Mrs. Hudson to the first coach as she was looking behind her. Then he saw a naked and bleeding Flora being dragged from the house by her arms. Her head was hanging down and she could not stand on her own. Billy wanted to run right to her and help her, but he knew better. He was the one that had to report to Sherlock how both women were coming out of the Brigadier's house. And he would do just that. He waited until he saw them roughly throw Flora into the coach as hands reached out to pull her in. Then he ran. Pumping his legs for all they were worth, tears streaming out behind him, he ran. And he was screaming though he wasn't aware of that.

Gregson was at the Brigadier's house. He saw too. He, like Billy, had to restrain himself. The big picture, he thought. We must get all these fiends. He wiped his eyes with the back of his hand, and he counted the eight full coaches headed hopefully to Ledingford's home. He sent a few irregulars to run to the men on the three routes they had staked out. Three coaches left before the first coach with the ladies in it, then the rest followed. Gregson made his way to a police vehicle and headed out to pick up men on the routes not taken then he would meet up at Ledingford's with Lestrade and tell him what he had seen.

Lestrade heard the coaches before he saw them. He and his men were well hidden. He had a good view of the coaches as they pulled up but not of the discharging of passengers. He would have to wait for Gregson to report on that. The coaches disgorged their passengers one by one, and as the people entered the house, the coaches and horses headed to the stables behind the house. Lestrade checked with his men to see if they were ready for the first watch. By the time he finished, Gregson was pulling up with his wagon and more officers who exited and took up their positions, watching the house from every angle.

Gregson looked a mess. Lestrade asked him what the matter was with him. He struggled getting words out at first. He was gulping air and tears began. Lestrade waited. He had seen this before. Men of his who had witnessed something traumatic. Finally, Gregson spoke, "I saw her. I saw her. I saw her when they brought her out. My god. Oh my god. She was naked and bleeding all over. She was unconscious, and they were dragging her by her arms. They threw her in the coach. Mrs. Hudson came out before her with what was left of her bodice in disarray, and they were pulling her to the coach as she was trying to get to Flora to help her. I'll never forget seeing that. Someone needs to tell Holmes.". He stood tall, and his eyes opened wider. "Billy, my god, Billy saw that. We need to get to Baker Street now." They grabbed a wagon, turned the horses, and headed to Baker Street.

Chapter 39

And Now Sherlock Knows

Billy entered 221b and flew up the 17 steps. Holmes and I heard him. He was screaming, but his voice was practically gone, like he'd been screaming for a long time. He ran to Holmes and threw his arms around him. Holmes tried to calm him but was having no luck. "Watson!" Holmes yelled. I tried to get Billy to let go but to no avail. "Holmes, I'm going to have to sedate him. We will learn nothing from him." Holmes was annoyed at this because it would have been the first word from anyone, but after feeling Billy shaking as he was holding him, he understood what he had seen was traumatic. Lestrade wouldn't let either of us be there at either house tonight in case they were watching us. It could get Mrs. Hudson, and Flora, killed. Holmes regretted that now.

I went for my bag. I heard commotion as I was coming from my room. Lestrade and Gregson had entered the flat and Gregson was now holding Billy in his arms. Billy was deathly quiet. I prepared a sedative and Gregson held Billy's arm as I injected him. I laid Billy on the sofa where he could be monitored and covered him gently.

We sat and Gregson began. "Sherlock, Billy saw what I saw and when I tell you what it was, you'll understand how he's going to be when he wakes up. First, Mrs. Hudson and Flora made it to Ledingford's. When they left, Mrs. Hudson was the first to come out. She was half naked and exposed at the top of her bodice, two men had her arms and she kept trying to look behind her, but they kept pulling her. Then I saw Flora. Holmes, steady yourself. She was naked and badly bleeding. She took a brutal beating and whipping and she was also raped because I saw blood coming down from between her legs. She was unconscious, her head was hanging down, and she was being dragged by her arms. They threw her in the coach. I'm sorry, Sherlock."

Holmes immediately stood. He walked to the window and stared out at the city. He turned and went to Billy. He knelt and wiped Billy's brow. "I'm so sorry lad. You are a very brave boy." He stood and asked Lestrade if he saw her leaving the coach. Lestrade said no. Then he said, "if you, gentlemen, excuse me for a few moments." He went into his and Flora's bedroom and quietly shut the door.

We were quiet, the rest of us, and after checking Billy, I poured us drinks, large ones. Then we sat quietly and waited for Holmes to come back out to us. I checked Billy again after about another 30 minutes had passed, and soon after the bedroom door opened, Holmes returned to his chair. He looked at us and said to Lestrade, "is there any way to expedite this?"

"Between the Yard and the Met, we may have a bare minimum, maybe enough, maybe not, and it's your brother Mycroft that we need to wait on as well," said Lestrade. "He knows the timetable for the foreign guests of Ledingford's as well as the police and government agency people from the three other countries involved. I think we need to let this play out the way we've planned. I know how horrible that sounds, Sherlock, but Flora is tough and smart. We expected this. I know it's different now that it's happened, but we need to trust her to hold everything together until two nights from now. I think we need to plan our entry into Ledingford's home. I know you have a set of plans to the home too. Let's compare notes."

I knew what Lestrade was doing. He was giving Holmes a task. Holmes probably knew, too, but I'm sure he was grateful for the distraction. We spread both sets of plans out on the table and began to compare notes.

Chapter 40

Aftermath

Flora woke to pain and cold. She was covered by two thin blankets. Mrs. Hudson was sitting on the edge of the cot Flora was on with her bodice open to her navel and buttons gone. She was covered, but barely. The only part of Flora that was warm was her hand, which Mrs. Hudson was gently holding in hers. She struggled to focus, and Mrs. Hudson said, "Flora, don't move. We don't know if you have broken bones. It's best you stay still." I turned my head, causing much pain, to see more of where we were. We were in another huge ballroom with sconces around the walls. Cots filled the wall on one side. On that other side, it looked like a torture chamber. Women were chained to the wall. Some dressed, some naked. The butterflies and moths.

There were beds on that side of the wall too. Men and women were in a few of them. The men were brutalizing the women. But the women were practically silent. They were moving along with the men and making forced sounds of pleasure, but I knew they were drugged. Some women were allowed to dress after the men were finished. The butterflies, drugged and addicted to laudanum. They were then chained to the wall again. Some were not allowed to dress, and either other men came to use them, or they were moved to the cots and chained there, still naked but witha thin blanket. Then a man would come to them, apply a tourniquet on their arms, and inject them. I counted the naked women. There were seven of them. There were about thirteen clothed women. I closed my eyes.

When I awakened again, Thomas was sitting on the bed. He had his hands under my blanket, caressing my breasts and when he saw me open my eyes, he pinched my breasts with his fingers until I screamed. "Ah, my moth still responds to my touch. Do you like my lepidoptery house? We do enjoy collecting. We take pleasure in ripping the wings off our specimens and pinning them. I don't suppose you recognize your friend Rose. She is over in the third bed with a member of parliament and his member right now. And the pretty little thing we took by mistake was a virgin. I took her like I took you years ago. I watched the pain in her eyes as I took her virginity as I took yours. A pretty thing indeed. Oh, and Mrs. Hudson is busy now. She is not on her cot." My eyes flew open! "No! No, I would never harm her unless you cause me to. I allowed her to use our facilities. I'm not a complete monster yet. My men became carried away with watching you suffer while they took turns with you and I'm afraid they ripped Mrs. Hudson's bodice as they played with her. I am allowing her to fix it."

I looked up at him and tried not to show the complete disgust I had for him. I wanted to ask him why he was doing this, but I couldn't speak. Thomas saw me try and said, "oh, my moth, do not try and talk. I choked you until you passed out several times last night. I'm afraid too hard. It was jolly good fun for me. But the doctor said you have vocal cord damage. Your screaming at my touch will do rather more harm than good, I'm afraid, so please try and control your lust and want for me. Ah, here comes Mrs. Hudson now. See, she's all put back together. I shall leave you alone for a while longer before my friends need you to relieve their tension."

"Flora, I heard you scream. Did he hurt you again?" I shook my head yes at her question. She had brought back a glass of water and gave me some. I whispered to her, "did you get a look to see if there are guards?"

"No guards and we are in the back of the house because there is a door to the garden behind a tapestry at the far end of the ballroom. I also saw some men playing cards in a side room. The kitchen has two cooks and a scullery that I saw. They wouldn't even look at me. There is a dining room that is being set for dinner. You were asleep all day. That means our rescue is tomorrow night. We must think of a way to keep him away from you until then. I think I know how. I'll tell him you began your monthly. Men, even men like him, are squeamish about that."

I looked at her and smiled. I thought it couldn't hurt, but probably wouldn't work. I shook my head yes. She said, "good, I saved some cloths they gave me last night to clean you up. I'm going to go tell him and ask for more cloths. If it works, we need just wait for the rescue. My dear, please try to sleep some more. You are deathly pale."

Sometime later, I awakened to find Thomas and Mrs. Hudson standing next to my cot. "Mrs. Hudson tells me I cannot take you to my bed tonight. I will give you two nights and then I will have you no matter what. There are other orifices I can use. Besides, I was quite rough with you last evening. I used techniques on you we use on moths we are getting ready to unpin. You will be happy to know they are effective. We do not set moths free. Ask Mrs. Hudson. One technique I used on you made her faint in her chair." He then took straps from under each side of the cot and strapped me to it so tightly that I winced in pain. He left smiling.

I motioned Mrs. Hudson over to me and kissed her cheek.

Chapter 41

Planning a Rescue

Holmes sent a message to Mycroft through one of the irregulars. Several of them had come to check on Billy. He was carried down to his room in Mrs. Hudson's flat by Holmes. A couple of his closest friends were allowed to stay on a cot in his room with strict orders to come and get me as soon as he showed signs of waking; however, I expected him to sleep the night.

We went back to going over the rescue and arrest plans and when Mycroft arrived, we were having a bit of a disagreement on where we thought the women were held. Holmes thought they were in the ballroom because of space and the need to keep them in one room. Lestrade thought they were in the bedrooms on the upper floors to keep them out of sight.

Lestrade was saying, "Sherlock, listen, they will want the women as far from prying eyes as possible. The higher up, the better. Of course, that makes our situation in rescue and arrests much more difficult. But if we position men the right way, we can do it and lessen casualties, too.". He harrumphed and folded his arms.

Holmes, exasperated and worried about Flora, responded by saying, "Lestrade, while that is sound thinking, it is nonetheless wrong. The irregulars that scouted the home for me confirmed the women are in the ballroom. Dark curtains are blocking the ballroom windows as well as the double doors to the garden. One of the irregulars begged for food at the kitchen door. A scullery took pity on him and brought him in to feed. She had quite a loose tongue and in conversation, he found out that there were indeed women in the ballroom, they were on cots and apparently, the scullery told him they were 'bad women' who were servicing men to trade their way out of the country. With all persons in the ballroom, women to be rescued and men to be arrested, I believe that to be a bit easier strategically; however, it is much more dangerous for the women. This will take careful planning on all our parts."

Mycroft interrupted at this point. "Gentlemen, I do see the point for careful planning and I'm afraid I may have inadvertently made it worse. The police and government agents from all three countries want their people to be a part of the arrest teams, or they will claim no knowledge and accuse the UK of allowing the trafficking of women to their countries go on without their knowledge, but with ours. I have made it clear that one of their police and one of their agents may participate, but only as observers, going in after the scene is secured and taking part in the arrests and interrogations at the Yard. I have limited their mayhem to six, but there you have it.". Holmes sat in his chair and lit his pipe, facing himself away from the rest of us.

Chapter 42

Doctor in Ordinary to the Queen

I awakened the next morning knowing that tonight Sherlock would be coming for us. I felt more awake this morning because the pain was a bit less and my brain could think through it. I looked over at Mrs. Hudson. She was sleeping on her cot and was not chained or strapped into it. I'm glad Thomas did not do that to her, but I know he realized that she would not abandon me here. My ankle was chained to the cot, and I was still strapped down. I could hear sounds of sex across the room and thought of those poor women. It seems Thomas was correct when he said they were used day and night. I shifted my weight and realized I needed to use the chamber pot. I didn't want to wake Mrs. Hudson.

An older gentleman seemed to materialize out of the gloom and almost darkness of the ballroom and he walked to my cot. He pulled a chair up next to me and introduced himself as a doctor. He said he had examined me after I arrived here from the Brigadier's home. I shuddered at the memory of that night. So much pain. I wasn't drugged, but it was still a blur though I remembered the pain Thomas inflicted on me for hours. He said, "you have, at my best guess, several broken ribs. Your vocal cords are damaged, and I prefer you use them as little as possible. You have kidney damage, and I'm afraid I will need you to use the chamber pot so I can see if you are still bleeding from them. You have many tears to your anus and bodily functions will be painful for a few weeks. I regret to have to tell you that the force and brutality Thomas used with you might have damaged you internally. I mean your womb. There is no way of knowing unless you are unable to conceive. Have you been pregnant before?" I shook my head, yes and the doctor continued. "Well then, if you do not conceive from here forward, you will know why. I did an internal examination upon your arrival. You were bleeding quite badly. I was able to stop some of it, but I fear the damage might have already been done. I'm sure your companion, Mrs. Hudson, is it?, has already suspected this. She would not let me examine you alone. Thomas is quite hard on his moths. He was particularly hard on you. He caused the internal damage purposely. He came close to choking the life out of you several times during the night at the Brigadier's. He also gave you quite a beating with his boots and fists before he began using you. I assume you had a past with him because of your treatment and the fact he said he is keeping you here in his London collection for his personal use and that of his old university mates. Beware of him, Miss James.

I'm no saint and I use the women he procures, but never the way he and his friends do. They are a rough lot who profess they haven't killed women because they are better alive for their pleasure, but that is a lie. There were 13 or more women here not a month ago. Now, let's get these off you so you can use the chamber pot. Please remember, if you do anything other than use the pot and return to your cot, Mrs. Hudson will suffer. Thomas has said at your first indiscretion, she will become a moth and he will use her in front of you. So, keep that in mind, please, because he never says anything he won't do."

The doctor released all my straps and took off the ankle cuff and placed them under the cot. He pulled out the chamber pot and pushed it close to the wall. He uncovered me and I shivered. I looked at my body and I gasped. There were cuts, scrapes, lumps, and swollen bruises everywhere I could see. There was dried blood and fresh blood running down my legs, both front and back. The doctor helped me use the wall for balance until I was able to use the pot. I no longer felt embarrassed. I was numb. He helped me back to bed and covered me. Each step I took was pain filled and I felt like I was smothering because I had to breathe so shallowly from the broken ribs. He said, "I see Mrs. Hudson gave her blanket to you. I will see she gets one for herself.". He looked into the chamber pot. "You are still bleeding from your kidneys. Please eat and drink all they feed you. I will see that you have a water pitcher." He stood and disappeared back into the gloom of the ballroom.

Mrs. Hudson sat up and came to my bed. "My sweet Flora. I heard the doctor and yes, I knew. When I saw Thomas hurt you like that, I fainted. I fear for these women and the others they might have already taken to the other countries. They will be, they are, suffering greatly just because they are women. I saw them feed their wives laudanum. First, they made them watch the other women as they were being used. Then the men used them in the same way until they begged for more laudanum. They addicted these women at home only to do this to them as they suffered withdrawal. Sinful."

My mind was now on overload. I couldn't process any more pain, physically or mentally.

Suddenly, I was blinded by light pouring into the ballroom. All the curtains were being opened and I could see the women. Pale, emaciated, bruised and bloodied like me. The wives were unchained and removed from the room. At least a dozen women in maid's uniforms came into the room and began cleaning, replacing chamber pots, changing cot linens, and replacing blankets with quilts. The kitchen staff came in and brought food to the seven women chained to cots, to Mrs. Hudson, and to me. The women ate as though ravenous. Though I was not hungry, Mrs. Hudson reminded me what the doctor said, and I dutifully ate. Curtains were closed again but not the curtains by the doors to the garden. The room had some natural light and all the sconce candles were replaced. There were gardeners outside and I could see them getting the garden ready to host guests that might want to step outside for a breath of air. The traffickers. All of us except Mrs. Hudson were given red blankets for our beds. In my mind, I thought what a bad colour choice, but in several hours, it wouldn't matter except to protect the women's modesty a bit.

Mrs. Hudson, after making sure I had eaten enough, tucked me in my cot and told me to see if I could sleep. She said, "Sherlock will be here with Scotland Yard and Doctor Watson, a real doctor. We will see what he says after we are safe in Baker Street again." She was shaking her head as if the doctor who saw me was a quack. He was not. I recognized him. He was the Queen's doctor. The doctor in ordinary to the Queen.

Chapter 43

Sherlock Says Thank You

Everyone was looking at the map now. With Holmes and Lestrade on the same page, the work of planning became easier. "Lestrade," said Holmes, "if we team two of your men with one from the Metropolitan police, then we can enter from the two back garden entrance doors and set them up to catch men attempting to leave through the garden. We are estimating approximately 70 men between club members and foreign co-conspirators. There may be more, but I feel that Thomas won't like to overwhelm his guests. He's selling this idea as much as running it as his club. There will be more arrests in the future, but I think we are safe to go with that number for now. We may hear differently, but we will worry about that then."

Lestrade agreed and said, "I'll also put two teams just outside the garden gates in case there's a stampede out the garden windows. I'll have a few wagons with guards out there as well. We will have two teams knock at the front double doors and keep them open for several more teams to enter and head to the ballroom. The remaining teams entering after that will disperse throughout the house and make further arrests. Once the upper floors are cleared, those teams will assist the others in the ballroom and garden. Sherlock, Doctor Watson, I will let both of you decide where you wish to enter but make it known to the teams so we don't have any that don't know the both of you trying to arrest you."

Then Holmes shocked us all when he said he would already be inside. "Mycroft was able to get me an invitation as an interested foreign dignitary. I will be leaving for the Savoy shortly, where I will be picked up by a carriage sent by Ledingford. Watson has agreed to have a locum he knows stay with Billy in case he wakes. Watson will come in with the last groups of police to enter and he will head straight to the ballroom. There he will assess the women and have them transferred to the police wagons to go to the hospital. He has also gotten St Bart's to be on standby to receive and treat the women as a priority. I have advised the booksmith from Whitechapel to check to see if his daughter is at St. Bart's in the morning. It will be a bittersweet welcome for them, I'm sure. Gentlemen, this will be a very dangerous task indeed. My future wife is in there holding all this together for us at a great personal cost. We will all be taking our places soon. I sometimes forget to thank the ones who help me the most, so I am thanking everyone now. We need to get the women to a hospital, these men arrested and charged, and Mrs. Hudson and Flora back home where they belong. I am grateful for all that you are doing to help me accomplish that task." Holmes then shook everyone's hand a picked up the bag he had packed earlier; then he left for the Savoy.

Chapter 44
This is Bad

Flora was awake and watching the light fade outside the garden windows. Fires had been made and between the fires and the quilts, the women were warmer than they had been in a long time. The sounds of sex were absent as well. Though getting dark, the room was now well-lit and comfortable. Flora was in pain, but it was now more bearable. She had not been strapped to her cot, so Mrs. Hudson helped her sit a few times for as long as she could stand it. She felt her strength returning and, with that, an anger towards these men. She wondered when Sherlock would arrive. She had no doubt that Mycroft had procured an invitation for him. He would, of course, be in disguise, but she would know him.

Mrs. Hudson had taken a nap as well and was awake now and watching two bar areas being set up on each side of the doorway into the ballroom. Glasses were tinkling. Bottles were being set. Mrs. Hudson thought that the men must be coming soon and they would be rescued after that. She thought what a high price Flora had paid for this. She wondered how Sherlock would react to Thomas not just having his way with her but beating her bad enough to cause internal injuries to her womb. Of course, he would love Flora just the same. If it were true that Flora couldn't have children, he would not be much bothered. He was not keen on children except the irregulars. But he would be very angry at Thomas and these men for taking away her choice over her own body. She had seen Sherlock very angry, and she feared it. She didn't want him to get into trouble he couldn't get out of. She heard Flora wince and turned to her.

"Flora, wait, let me help you." Flora was returning to her cot from using the chamber pot. Mrs. Hudson looked in it and noticed much less blood. "Your kidneys seem to be getting better with this uninterrupted bed rest. I'm glad our ruse worked on him. I don't think I could bear watching him hurt you again. I'm sure it's getting near the time when the men are coming and we will soon be done with this awful place and back in Baker Street. I can tell you it's none too soon for me."

I looked at Mrs. Hudson and smiled. Right to the point, even in a dire situation like this. "Mrs. Hudson, I haven't addressed this yet because my mind has been a jumble and I've been in much pain. But I saw what they did to you that first night. I saw them tear your bodice open and touch you intimately. No one should be subjected to being touched against their will like that, least of all you. I'm so very sorry."

"Flora," said Mrs. Hudson softly. "It isn't the worst thing that has ever happened to me. Hopefully, it will be the last. To be honest, I don't remember much of it because I was concentrating on the brutal things Thomas was doing to you while those men just watched and played with themselves in their drawers like naughty little boys while waiting their turn."

As soon as Mrs. Hudson stopped speaking, I noticed the maids came in again to straighten up and change chamber pots. They came back with thin pillows for the seven women, Mrs. Hudson, and me. They returned once again and sprayed the quilts over us with a floral perfume. As soon as they left, several men came in. Thomas's men. They went to the seven women, tied tourniquets on their frail arms, and injected them. Even the young girl accepted the narcotic mix willingly and with a smile. Within a few minutes, they were well into feeling the drug laced with Thomas's mixture. They began rubbing and touching themselves under their quilts and moaning with self-pleasuring. The aphrodisiac was working in them. A show for the men who would probably be encouraged to rape them.

Mrs. Hudson and I were so unaware of our surroundings in watching of the poor women that we did not see Thomas and William approach us with a tray. Startled, I said, "surely you are not doing this to us too! Thomas, not to Mrs. Hudson! Please! Please don't humiliate her like that."

He smiled and shook his head, "No, moth, I would not do that, but I am feeding her a nice big healthy dose of laudanum. Did you know she was an addict too? Did she or Sherlock ever tell you that? No, I can see by the look on your face. Shame on you, Mrs.

Hudson. I can tell you she loved her laudanum so much she would do anything for it. No matter what it was. Both of you will take your first steps back to your addictions right now." He turned to Mrs. Hudson. "William has a nice healthy and large dose of laudanum for you. Drink it and you will not get a needle with my concoction in it. It doesn't matter to me what you choose. Oh, and this evening you are to be sold to our Russian collection. They do not care about age when they give women to their soldiers. Sadly, you will not live long, they use whores harder than even I do, but you will die knowing you made some foreign soldiers happy." William held the glass out to Mrs. Hudson, who had begun crying. She just stood there. Paralyzed in fear. William grabbed her hair and pulled her head back and poured the contents of the glass down her throat and pushed her roughly into her cot.

Thomas had been holding me and I was still struggling to get to Mrs. Hudson. He and William held me down, put a tourniquet on my arm, and administered the drug to me. He said, "this is not my concoction, my moth, just opium. A good dose of it mixed with morphine, enough that in a few minutes, you won't even miss Mrs. Hudson after she's sold this evening. Nothing will matter but the drug. You will be a good little moth and we will see that you have it. After dinner tonight, the men we are entertaining will entertain you, my love. Then you will get my special mix."

I turned to see Mrs. Hudson smiling a blank smile. The drug

making her forget everything, even who she was or where she was going. Then, my body was wracked by tremors, and I became oblivious to the world outside the pleasure of the drug coursing through me and giving me blissful peace.

Sherlock's thoughtful interlude......

The coach arrived at the Savoy to pick up Mr. Richard Brook, the name I was using once again. I stepped into the opulent coach and began to form a plan for the evening. There were still too many variables to formulate a solid plan. I don't like that; things fall apart when there are too many unknowns. I knew I had a thirty-minute ride at minimum, so I explored possibilities in my mind palace. First, the worst. Flora and Mrs. Hudson could be dead or gone already. I doubt both. They were too valuable to kill and again too valuable to take anywhere else when he was showing off his collection to the buyers he hoped would join his plan and thereby make him money, sex trafficking unfortunates and other poor women. Then I thought the women might have been moved to a different part of the home. I could possibly get word to Lestrade and Gregson by stepping outside for a breath of air and attracting the attention of an irregular. They knew my shorthand signs and could tell the inspectors what they needed to know. There could be guards now. The irregulars had said there were none earlier, but that could change. That might complicate things and present a clear danger to the women. I could be recognized. That would indeed cause a problem. One that would be dangerous to Flora and Mrs. Hudson, as well as myself. As I was running all these possibilities in my mind, the coach approached Lord Ledingford's home and came to a stop. The game begins.

Chapter 45

Sherlock in the Lion's Den

The doors to the home were opened by butlers in a white glove. A maid stood by the door with glasses of champagne on a tray. I passed her by. The foyer was large and many men were mingling and admiring the surroundings. Most were drinking champagne, and several had had more than enough from the sound of their slurred speech. I noticed double doors across from the main doors that had heavy drapes across them. The ballroom. I got as close as I could, but it was impossible to see inside. I walked through the crowd again, recognising many of the men I saw. Just as I suspected, there were many men from Lestrade's list too. A door opened to our right and a butler announced dinner was served. We entered the lavish dining room, where butlers and servers were standing behind chairs to seat us. I was seated across from Thomas and next to his university friend Lord William Frake. Dinner was served and I made my way through eating as little as I could. I can't bear eating whilst on a case. As the fruit and cheese were being served, Thomas stood and spoke to us.

"Gentlemen, I am glad to see you all here tonight. The seven women I have here tonight are up for bid to take to your own lepidoptery clubs. I expect more shortly, and you may also tell us what you are looking for. We can fulfil most requests. For example, our Russian club requested an older woman we happen to have for their soldiers. As we have one here tonight, they will be able to leave with her. She has been drugged with laudanum already, and if requested, she can be medicated with my mix that I have already shared with every club. I have medicated the seven with this mix. You can observe the effects when we enter my pinning room. There have been fully stocked bars set up for your pleasure. I have my special moth here tonight and will inject her in front of you so you can see my mix work from the first few minutes. We do have a very special treat this evening. Quite unexpected. I will be bedding my moth in front of her intended husband."

I was startled by that statement and felt a sting in my neck and my world went blank. I awoke tied to a chair in the ballroom. I was in front of a cot with Flora in it. She, too was coming out of a drugged stupor. Next to her was a cot with laudanum drugged Mrs. Hudson. There was a tag on her cot that said sold in big red letters. I could hear men engaged in what could only be sex across the room behind me. Thomas stepped into my vision. William was with him, and he held a tourniquet and syringe. He tied the tourniquet on Flora's arm and looked at Thomas. Thomas was gloating over this. He said to Sherlock, inches from his face, "did you think with a spy in government, we wouldn't know you were coming? We knew not five minutes after your brother agreed to your coming and received an invitation for you. Now, just look at your lovely Flora. This isn't just opium in the syringe, it's a mix that will make her want sex with anyone. And when I inject her, I will make you watch as I take her. Then I will have anyone that wants her to take her like the moth she is. You will watch all of it. Our members are brutal with moths. You should have quite the show" I was struggling against the ropes holding me. Thomas said, "the minute he looks away from Flora or closes his eyes, William, would you be good enough to slit Mrs. Hudson's throat, please." William sat on the cot with Mrs. Hudson and took out a knife that was the twin of the one left in Flora that first night she arrived at my flat. He lifted her head and placed it in his lap. With one hand, he held the knife across her neck, and with the other, he reached into her bodice and stroking her, evoking soft mewling noises from Mrs. Hudson. I was outraged.

I looked at Flora, helpless to stop what was happening. There was a contingent of men in various stages of undress that gathered around and watched and waited for their turn with Flora. Thomas came over to me and whispered in my ear, "you will slowly lose your mind watching the ways we will rape your future wife. You'll never be able to solve another case again. Your brain will be able to think of nothing else. We will use her in every way, and she will love it and beg for more, thanks to my drug." I have never wanted to do to another man what was in my head to do to Thomas. He pulled Flora's legs up and ripped the quilt from the cot. I wanted to look away, but I couldn't. Flora's body had been ravaged. I could see bruises and boot marks, lines from whips crossed her body, the first marks and bruises showing where she was hit. Blood was coming from her and soaked into the cot.

Seeing him about to take away her consent with drugs as he poked the syringe into her swollen vein brought out an anger in me I've never had before. I yelled at him to stop, begged him not to do anymore to her, and the men around me laughed and asked Thomas for turns with Flora. Some bid on her for their own clubs. I couldn't stand not being able to stop this. Tears sprung from my eyes, and then Thomas pushed the plunger. Everyone was silent. Flora looked at me as tears poured from her eyes. Then her body was wracked with tremors, and she began to move her hands over her naked body pleasuring herself. Men began moaning and touching themselves watching her and Thomas was looking at me, smiling.

"Sherlock, don't look away now. I want this burned in your brain." Thomas began caressing Flora's body and joining his hands with hers. I wanted to scream, but I couldn't. I felt my brain shutting down. My mind palace emptying of all except what I saw happening to my Flora. I was helpless to do anything other than watch as he took his fingers from her body and crawled onto her, entering her. I heard his moans of pleasure and they echoed in my brain slowly obliterating my mind and my heart. I saw him on her and I saw nothing else in the room. Then the glass of the ballroom's double doors burst, and police began entering. Thomas pulled himself from inside Flora's body and ran.

Chapter 46

The Rescue

Soon there was police everywhere and half-dressed men running wildly as they were intercepted and cuffed by the constables that flooded the ballroom. A few men resisted and regretted that decision. The police had seen the women and would gladly beat any man responsible for hurting them. Then, Watson was beside me. "Watson! Cover Flora and then check Mrs. Hudson. She's been drugged. And then get me out of these ropes."

Watson carefully covered Flora and went to Mrs. Hudson. "Holmes, she's been given laudanum. A good dose of it. She'll be out for a few hours more at least." He checked Flora. "Holmes, Flora has been given multiple doses of opium. Her breathing is laboured. She looks to have broken ribs and, most probably, internal injuries as well. She needs a hospital, and soon, or we may lose her."

Watson came to me and cut my bonds with his army knife. I ran to Flora and kissed her. I whispered I love you to her and looked around the room as I held her. Constables had arrested many of the men. Thomas was not among them. The women had been covered but were still in the throes of Thomas's drug. There were constables putting them onto stretchers and covering them carefully as though they might break.

I saw Lestrade and Gregson enter the ballroom. I called to Lestrade. "We need to get Flora to the hospital immediately. Watson said she is having trouble breathing. Lestrade called two constables over and asked them to get a stretcher and get Flora to a wagon, then take Flora to the hospital, top priority. Then he called a few others over and planned to get the women and Mrs. Hudson to the hospital on every available wagon. He said the cuffed men could sit on the floor of the ballroom until the wagons came back from the hospital run.

Lestrade turned to me and said, "Sherlock, this is a mess. There are foreign dignitaries that will probably have diplomatic immunity, but we will take them in and will process them. Gregson here had to arrest the Doctor in Ordinary to the Queen! We will have to let him go once we tell the Palace, I'm sure of that. Many of these men are Lords, bankers, barristers, and business owners. We did arrest the Brigadier as well. Mycroft will need to be told." I asked Lestrade, "Did you get Thomas and William?" He said they were looking, but they had not found them yet. He also said it would take hours to get the arrested men to the Yard and to be processed. All totalled, they had arrested sixty-three men.

Gregson, who had left the ballroom, came running back in. "No sign of the two Lords, but we just found a treasure trove of business plans for the trafficking ring. They've taken more than these seven women captives. But others have died because of their treatment. They've detailed it. All the brutal and disgusting things they did were written down, with names and dates too. Some of these men, including the two Lords, Ledingford and Frake, will be hung. If we find them. So far, we have not."

I went under Flora's now empty cot and grabbed the almost empty syringe and gave it to Gregson. "Here is more evidence. It's the drug that they were giving the women. There is enough left in it to use as evidence." Gregson took it carefully and removed a leather bag he had on his belt and placed the syringe inside. I asked Lestrade if Watson and I could leave for the hospital and go to Flora and Mrs. Hudson. He told us there was nothing left for us to do here, just Yard work and we took our leave.

The Keeper of the Flame

Moth, you have made me very angry. I have had to leave my ancestral home because of your meddlesome Consulting Detective. It's only a temporary setback, I assure you. The men arrested are inconsequential. There are always men who get off by hurting women. But my best friend, William, for that, you will both pay. The man isn't stable without the drugs I feed him. He can ruin me. If he tries to, I'll just have him killed. But you and your Sherlock. I shall capture both of you and make you bed each other for show. I shall charge a small fortune. And I will teach him how to hurt you. He'll want his drugs. He will do it. And my pet, I will not drug you. You will know your Sherlock wants something so much more than you that he will hurt the woman he loves to get it. I shall service him to men while you serve the onlookers drinks. I shall break you both for this. Then I shall kill both of you and feed you to wild beasts. I am coming for you moth. Fear not.

Chapter 47

The Hospital

Holmes was quite quiet on the ride to the hospital. A young constable was with us. He was to check on the women and try and to get names. I needed to check my patients, Mrs. Hudson and Flora. I knew Mrs. Hudson was an addict. This was a fact she shared with me when Holmes was deep into his 7 percent solution. The laudanum she received, if only once, would likely not lead her to relapse. And if she had not been touched by these men, then she should be fine in a couple of days. Flora, however, was in bad shape. I saw what they did to her by the story on her body. I knew she had been given large quantities of opium, in all probability, more than once. That was troubling but did not in and of itself mean she would relapse. But her mental state after this could mean that was a likely possibility. There were most definitely internal injuries. Her beating took place mainly between her pubis and navel. There were many boot marks there too. I knew the possibility of her uterus being damaged was high. It was as if Thomas was planning for that to happen. There were several broken ribs. I also knew I'd have a third patient, Holmes. I remember how I was with Mary when she fell ill. Holmes will be worse. Holmes just watched his future wife drugged and raped by a madman.

We approached the hospital and I asked immediately where

my patients were. I then headed to the correct ward with Holmes and the constable behind me. We checked on Mrs. Hudson first. She was awake and the attending doctor said she was fine. She saw us and said, "Doctor Watson, I'm fine. I need to see Flora and the other women and that poor young booksmith's daughter. Please don't make me sit in this bed and worry myself sick enough to be useless."

I couldn't help but realise there was no keeping her in that bed. "Mrs. Hudson, you may go to the women first; this constable will go with you. See if you can get names and next of kin if possible. I've yet to check Flora myself. You must wait to see her."

"Very well, Doctor Watson, I'll see what I can do. Please let me know as soon as I can see Flora." Mrs. Hudson sat and was straightening her clothes when I turned to her again.

"Mrs. Hudson, can you tell me what happened to Flora? I understand you were with her the entire time."

"Yes, Doctor Watson. That night at the Brigadier's was awful. I watched while Lord Ledingford slapped her to the ground and began kicking her in the stomach, the lower back, and then anywhere. He had her held whilst he beat her stomach. He had her on the floor and took her whilst choking her until she almost passed out. When he finished, he was handed a horsewhip and he beat her with it. She turned around and tried to crawl away and he mounted her and took her, well, not in a place where she could get pregnant.

Then he let anyone who paid him take her." Mrs. Hudson blushed and took a breath and continued. "He took her or beat her for hours and she was not drugged. He told her he wanted her to feel every brutal thing he and his cronies did and then be glad for the drug when he finally gave it to her. That's what he did to the other women when he first got them too. But the next day, I told him she was on her monthly and he didn't touch her. Men, even men like him, can be squeamish about a perfectly normal and natural occurrence. But then I was in and out after they forced me to drink laudanum. But Sherlock, I saw you tied to the chair; I heard him say what he was going to do to Flora in front of you. I hope you catch him and give him his knife back if you know what I mean." She turned and left for the women's ward with the constable.

Holmes and I entered a private room and saw Flora. She was also coming awake and saw Holmes and reached her hand out to him. He took it in his hands and kissed it over and over. Then he bent and kissed her forehead and her lips. He pulled a chair closer and sat next to her. I thought I would give them a minute and I went to find the attending that examined her.

I found Doctor Satti in the break room, and we sat. He began, "John, her injuries are many. Swelling, bruises, and abrasions all over her body. She was badly beaten. Her kidneys were damaged, but with time I think they will heal. She is still bleeding into her urine, but it is slight. Her rectal area is bruised and bleeding.

However, her womb area was the most badly damaged. I examined her internally and her womb was bleeding and misshapen from swelling and tears. I'm afraid she will no longer be able to have children. I know she is close to you. Would you like me to tell her and Mr. Holmes, or do you want to do that?" He reached out and put his hand on my arm in comfort. I hung my head so he wouldn't see my tears, then I said, "Imran, will you come with me to tell them?" He shook his head, yes and we headed to Flora's room.

Flora was sitting up and propped with pillows. Holmes was holding her hand. They looked up as we walked in. Flora said, "Sherlock, this is my doctor, Doctor Satti. Doctor, this is my soon-to-be husband, Sherlock Holmes." Holmes and Imran shook hands. I went and stood behind Holmes and put a hand on his shoulder. Imran began, "I have all the results of my examination of you, Miss James. You have many bruises, contusions, abrasions and cuts. All will heal just fine. You might be sore for a while; warm baths might help some areas. Warm compresses too. You have kidney damage, but that, too, will heal well. You know you took most of your beating in the area of your womb. I'm afraid that's been irreparably damaged. You will not be able to get pregnant, nor bear a child should that ever happen."

Flora froze in shock. Holmes, who still had her hand, pulled it to his heart and laid his head in her lap. He was sobbing. Flora, who was crying too, laid her head over his and held him with her other hand. Imran and I left the room and closed the door.

We met Mrs. Hudson in the hall. The constable was with her. She had been able to get their names and more and relatives were being notified. They would be hospitalized for a few weeks. They, too, were beaten, addicted, and used so brutally that we may have to do surgery on some of them. Imran went back to his rounds and the constable left to find Lestrade. I told Mrs. Hudson about Flora and she said she had guessed as much. I told her I had been with them when Imran told them. "No! Doctor Watson, you didn't leave them alone!" So back we went to Flora's room.

I knocked and opened the door slowly. Mrs. Hudson followed me in. Sherlock was in the chair, and you could see he had recently stopped crying. Flora still had tears in her eyes, but she, too, has stopped crying. I said, "So sorry to disturb you, but we were worried."

"Ah, dear Watson. Thank you. Flora and I talked. It was a shock, and we are both deeply saddened. She has known about my aversion to all children except the irregulars. She asked if it was the truth and of course, I told her yes. She is new to her career and wasn't sure she ever wanted children, either. Another way we are alike. However, we are both deeply upset. We were not given a choice about this. It was taken away from us. From Flora. Women suffer so much, Watson. They are called the weaker sex. They are often stronger than men and often smarter. Yet they are still abused for the pleasure of men. Their rights, what little they have, are all too often tread upon harshly. They don't even have rights to their children. Everything is stacked in the favour of males. Watson, we need to do more to help women, especially unfortunates and poorer women. In that regard, Flora has agreed to testify against these men. I'm sure Mrs. Hudson will as well."

Mrs. Hudson spoke up and said, "You can be sure of that, Sherlock."

Then Holmes said, "Watson, Mrs. Hudson, Flora and I wish to marry on Christmas day. Will the both of you stand up for us?"

I jumped up and grabbed Holmes' hand and said, "Holmes, old man, yes. I never thought I'd see the day. Yes, I'm proud and honoured to do so."

Mrs. Hudson went to Flora and hugged her. "Flora, of course, I'll stand up for you. We have bonded very much, and you are as my daughter. But a Christmas wedding, there are only four weeks to plan!"

I told Holmes I was keeping Flora at least overnight. Maybe another day or two after that. He understood. Flora did not, but with Holmes' urging, she acquiesced. The door opened again and the locum that had been watching Billy walked in with him in tow. The locum said he would not rest after a constable came and said all of you were here. I thanked him and said we would take care of Billy from here.

Billy walked up to the side of the bed and put his head down. He said, "I saw." With his gravelly voice still hoarse from screaming. "Oh Billy, said Flora, "I'm so very sorry you saw that, but I'm fine. Sometimes fighting for what you believe in is hard and you get hurt. But it's worth it in the end because you save lives and protect people's rights. Do you understand?" Billy said he thought he did. Then Flora said, "Billy, Sherlock and I are to marry on Christmas day. The irregulars are invited. Will you tell the others?" Billy was all smiles then and properly congratulated the happy couple. After they all made sure Billy was indeed fine, Mrs. Hudson said she was going home with him and that she would be waiting for Holmes and me to return there as soon as we were able. They said their goodbyes and left. I told Holmes I was making rounds on the women as Lestrade had sent a message to me that he needed medical diagnoses on the seven that were here, but I would be back to take him home when I was finished. He thanked me for giving him more time with Flora, and I quietly left the room.

The attendings had already checked all seven women. They all were addicted and would need to go through withdrawals from the drugs. Some of them were so badly hurt that they would not be able to live through it. We would see they were as comfortable as possible until they gave up their fight. The young girl, who we now know is Anna Lindt, will be checked for pregnancy. Though it was early, she had certain internal changes that made the doctor suspect. The women were not just raped, they were tortured as well. Many had the same strangulation marks on their necks that Flora had, including her friend Rose. She was treated brutally, indeed. Like Flora, she would never bear children. Her kidneys were also damaged from beatings, but hers were not healing yet. If she didn't improve soon, her last days would be spent in this hospital. I gathered all the information that Lestrade requested and called the hospital messenger. After I made rounds of my own to several of my regular patients who were here, I returned to Flora's room.

Flora was sleeping and Holmes was just staring at her. He looked at me when I entered and pulled a chair up next to him. "Watson," he began, "when I was tied in that chair and forced to look at Flora and see what they had done to her, and hear from that monster's lips what he was going to do, what he did do to her taking her body with his as I watched, I feared I would go insane. Thomas said that to me. He said that I would go insane and never solve another case. I have lost some of my mind. I fear he was correct. I can't stop seeing it in my brain. I can't think of anything else. It replay's over and over in my head. Watson, am I going insane?" Holmes looked beaten. There were dark circles under his red-rimmed eyes.

"Holmes, any man would go a bit insane seeing what you

179

did. You were traumatized. You will see what you saw even in your dreams, I'm afraid. But your mind will heal with time. As Flora gets well, so will you. For now, don't fight those feelings or what you see. But don't let them consume you either. I am arranging for you and Flora as well as Mrs Hudson and Billy to talk to a psychiatrist. I've advised Lestrade to arrange this for Gregson as well. For now, ground yourself in the knowledge Flora is safe and you, my dear Holmes, are lucky enough to be marrying this lovely, wonderful, brave, and amazing woman in a month. My dear Holmes, I would be worrying more about planning a wedding. But on that note, I sent Lestrade the information he requested. I also received a note that they apprehend William, Lord Frake, and he is now a blithering idiot. Apparently, Thomas was drugging him too. Though he was probably using drugs himself for a long time, Thomas became his supplier. He is heavily in withdrawal and speaking like a jaybird. This operation they concocted is a large one indeed. And he knows everything. They have not found Thomas, so Lestrade is posting two guards here with Flora and four guards at Baker Street, front and back." With that, Flora's guards showed up and greeted Holmes and me. At Holmes' request, one will stay in the room and sit with Flora. He didn't want her to wake alone. He also didn't want to leave her tonight, but I insisted. He needed to check Mrs. Hudson and Billy himself and he needed rest badly. He broached little argument. And we headed back to 221b Baker Street.

Chapter 48

Mrs. Hudson and Lestrade

When Holmes and I reached the top of the seventeen steps and opened the door, there was a wonderful and warm fire blazing in the fireplace. The table was set and a roast chicken with potatoes, carrots and gravy was setting, steaming hot, on the sideboard. There was a nice pot of tea and four place settings. Mrs. Hudson and Billy stood there smiling. I said, "This looks absolutely delicious. I'm quite hungry myself. What say you, Holmes, didn't Mrs. Hudson outdo herself?"

Holmes looked at the food like it wasn't even there, but he managed a smile and politely sat. "Mrs. Hudson, it smells wonderful," he said, "I think I am hungry, actually. Let's eat, shall we?"

Mrs. Hudson poured the tea and we all sat and shared a truly delicious meal together. As we finished and Holmes and I had our cigar and pipe, Mrs. Hudson spoke about the events, which we had avoided all throughout the meal. "Sherlock, I don't want you to feel badly on my account. I'm sure Flora already told you about herself. I knew that this would be dangerous and that I would be hurt. I understood the risks. I wanted to do it. Inspector Lestrade came by earlier to check on me. He said this trafficking ring was in three countries and fully set up. He said there were girls there already. He said that Thomas and his cronies were setting up more clubs in England and there were plans to take young girls from the countryside as there was a demand for virgins. That's horrendous. But I can sleep better at night knowing I had a part in stopping it. Women are not things created for men's pleasure. We are equals. We are partners, and we are capable too. Trafficking women, and children as well, must be stopped. We are all responsible for our fellow man and woman. We all must put an end to this together." She shook her head and folded her arms.

"Well said, Mrs. Hudson," I stated

Holmes held his pipe and said, "I cannot imagine men who want to do things so degrading to another human being. While, for the most part, I ignored the fairer sex, except for you, Mrs. Hudson, and now Flora, and to a lesser degree, Irene Adler, I would never think to abduct, rape, and torture a woman. This case is difficult because men can't think like that for the most part. We knew our best bet was to use women to help with this case. They could understand being treated like that. Even if they hadn't been, they know women who have been. Women are not well treated in society overall. They are thought of as less than others. They are regulated by men in all they do. Their minds, their bodies, and custody of their children all ruled by men. I wish to see a society that respects their women. That gives them free control of their minds and bodies. The right to choose if they want children or not. They bear them. It's their bodies. It's their choice. We force so much on and yet take so much from women. Mrs. Hudson, I truly appreciate you. I am amazed by your quiet strength, your courage, and the abilities that make you stand out. Your ability to put up with Watson and me through the years and yet feed us like kings is brilliant. Thank you. And I respect you for knowing you had to subject yourself to harm to right a wrong being done to your sisterhood."

Mrs. Hudson had a hanky to her eyes, and she reached out and took Holmes' hand and gave it a squeeze. "Bravo, Holmes," I said. Billy sat quietly, holding his hands in his lap and wringing them. Holmes got up from his chair and knelt by him. "Billy, I know you saw a lot. I saw Flora like that too." Billy looked at him shaking his head.

"No, Sherlock, it's not Flora. I saw that she was okay. It's what Mrs. Hudson said about helping and what you said about rights and wrongs. A lot happens to us poor kids too. We get beat. We get laughed at. If we had family, they would have it hard too. But one of the irregular's mother's had a baby. She left it in the carriage to go sees if she could have the day-olds in the grocers. When she came out, the baby was gone. It's happened to a few babies; they get missing sometimes if you are poor. Can you help Sherlock?"

"Billy, I shall make it my next case after this one is finished.

I promise.". Billy smiled and hugged him. Holmes, who usually did not like displays of affection, hugged him back.

We all helped clean up and as we were sitting down to relax a bit before going to bed, Lestrade and Gregson knocked, and Billy brought them up. Lestrade said, "Here is where we stand in this case, Sherlock. We had to let the Doctor in Ordinary go with no charges. But we knew that. Mycroft is working on those claiming diplomatic immunity. There were eighteen foreign guests. When deaths are involved, that can be circumvented. We arrested twelve Lords, all seated in parliament. Five bankers of the top banks in London. Ten were businessmen, including the owner of the Lepidoptery shop in London. You know we arrested Lord Frake. But Lord Ledingford still alludes capture. It's a matter of time. All outlets from London and indeed the country are aware of him and looking for him. Within a few weeks we'll have him. And we have so much evidence against all of them that with written statements from you, Doctor Watson, Mrs. Hudson, and Miss James, I don't think we will need in-person testimony; statements should be sufficient. We will get statements from everyone during the next week

Holmes thanked him saying, "Thank you for this detailed update. I'm glad you do not need in-person testimony. We have all had enough of this. It had been difficult. But while you are both here, Flora and I have decided to marry on Christmas day. Will you both come and bring your wives?"

Gregson got up and shook Holmes' hand, congratulating him profusely. Lestrade said, "Well, I'll be damned. The great Sherlock Holmes, Consulting Detective, is going into domestic bliss!!! Sherlock, I wish you much love. You have a feisty and brave woman there. I know you'll treat her well and encourage her because she's one hell of a detective too."

"Lestrade, you are right," Holmes said, "Flora is indeed a good detective. We spoke about that at the hospital. And she will still be running her agency in Whitechapel with the help of Mrs. Hudson and the irregulars. I will assist if need be, but Watson and I have our own cases. I've just accepted a case from our Billy involving missing babies. This case will also require the assistance of Flora and Mrs. Hudson if we are to solve it. First though, I will marry and have a brief Brighton honeymoon."

The inspectors stayed for tea and as we all were tired, they left, and Billy and Mrs. Hudson returned to their flat. I insisted Holmes not stay up for a pipe but go to bed immediately. I also asked his door be left open until morning so I could hear if his sleep was interrupted by nightmares. Holmes acquiesced. I went up to my bedroom, assuring Holmes I would wake him if he wasn't awake when I came down for coffee.

Chapter 49

Planning a Wedding and Christmas

I was finally home! I was healing well though I would have scars from the beatings I had taken from that madman Thomas. I was back at 221b Baker Street and Mrs. Hudson was flitting over me like a bee to a flower. I was sitting on Sherlock's chair because he and Watson were out on a short case and were also planning to stop and check on the case we just solved. There were designs for wedding dresses on my lap. "Mrs. Hudson, I don't seem to like any of these. I've looked at so many. It's three weeks until the wedding. I'll never have a dress made in time between planning for this and planning for my first Christmas with all of you." I sat back and sipped my tea while trying to take another look at the gowns.

Mrs. Hudson said, "You know, my dear, I might have a solution to the dress for you. Please give me a few minutes." She stood and headed to the unused flat upstairs. Mrs. Hudson didn't need to rent it out, so it was used for storage. I could hear her moving boxes until, finally, she yelled "Aha!" and I heard her coming down the stairs.

Mrs. Hudson came bounding into the room with a large box. She held it as she said, "Flora, you don't have to like this, but as we were going over wedding gowns for the past several days, well, it came into my mind what you are looking for. This fits your description and with very little alterations, I think it will fit." She placed the box on the sofa and bade me come to her.

I lifted the lid and moved away the tissue paper. Inside was the most beautiful wedding gown I'd ever seen. I lifted it gently and held it in front of me. Mrs. Hudson gasped and said "Oh my, Flora, it's you!" I swirled, holding it in front of me. "Oh, Mrs. Hudson, this is indeed perfect. I love everything about it." The gown was a creamy pearl white. It had long sleeves that came to a point on the hand with a finger loop. The neckline was a take on the sweetheart neckline but slightly different. The gown hugged the body until it was slightly below the waist, where it flared out, but less than a ballroom gown would. The bustle was a French one. The whole gown was beaded with pearls and tiny rhinestones in tiny rosebuds, but not garishly so. When the light hit the gown, it sparkled. It was exquisite. The veil was as long as the train on the gown, chapel length. It was held in place by a delicate pearl tiara. It was just what I had imagined I'd be married in one day. "Mrs. Hudson, wherever did you get this?"

"My dear one, it was mine when I married. I felt like a princess in it though I married a toad. But Sherlock is not a toad. You two are fated to be together. Come into the bedroom. Try it on so I can see how I need to alter it."

I took the gown and ran into the bedroom and doffed my clothes. I put on the gown and Mrs. Hudson fastened the intricate corset back. Sherlock had a full-length mirror and I stood before it speechless. I looked beautiful. Mrs. Hudson placed the tiara in my hair and anchored it. Suddenly, I couldn't breathe. I sank to the floor, gasping. Mrs. Hudson ran to me and patted my back gently. "Flora, was this another attack?" she asked.

"Yes, they are so unpredictable. The doctor calls them fainting spells, but they aren't. I don't faint. I just can't breathe; I feel my heart race. I panic. I think I'll call them panic attacks. That name fits better. But I'm fine now." I stood and looked in the mirror again. Mrs. Hudson came behind me and pulled the back a bit tighter. "You are a bit smaller than I was. I could take it in a bit on both sides," she said.

"No, please. It looks perfect and in three weeks, I shall hopefully gain the weight back I lost in the hospital. I don't want it changed. It's something borrowed, and I love it. It's very generous of you." Then we heard it! Sherlock and Doctor Watson are on the stairs. "Oh no, Mrs. Hudson, what do I do?" She told me to stay where I was and she left the bedroom and closed the door.

Mrs. Hudson intercepted Holmes and me on the stairs. She explained that Flora was trying on her wedding gown and Holmes could not see it. Holmes shrugged and said it was nonsense and Mrs.

Hudson said nonetheless, you will sit in your chair and stay out of the bedroom. But she asked me to accompany her for a second opinion. So, Holmes sat and I followed.

As I entered the bedroom and saw Flora standing there, I was left speechless. She was a vision. She looked like a princess. She gave me a soft smile and suddenly, I had tears in my eyes. It overwhelmed me. The thought of the last few weeks and the horror Flora went through and seeing her here now was too much for me. I went to her and hugged her. "Flora, you look beautiful. Holmes is a lucky man to have a beauty such as you to marry." I backed up and looked at the gown. It looked like I'd seen it before. Yes, in a painting in Mrs. Hudson's flat. A painting of her and her husband. They sat for it after their wedding day. Mrs. Hudson, is this your wedding gown?"

"Yes, Doctor Watson. Flora couldn't find anything she liked and it's just sitting in that box, so I thought it should get some more use. Do you approve?"

"Definitely, Mrs. Hudson. It looks lovely. When Sherlock sees it he will, of course, connect the dots faster than I did and he will appreciate it very much."

Mrs. Hudson then unceremoniously threw me out of the bedroom so Flora could change her clothes.

Chapter 50

The Wedding Gown

"Well," said Holmes as I sat and picked up a cigar. I looked at him and laughed a hearty laugh indeed. "Old man, I'll be picking you up off the altar floor. The people at the ceremony will see that Sherlock Holmes has a heart and he's not all a thinking machine." I continued laughing, which I could see upset Holmes, which in turn made me laugh harder.

"Watson, please control yourself; it is just a dress, after all." Homes shouted just as Mrs. Hudson and Flora were coming from the bedroom.

"Sherlock! Did I hear you call my wedding gown 'just a dress? I hope I heard you wrong. A wedding gown is a symbol. My cream gown symbolizes the goodness and innocence of the wedding vows. Different colour gowns have different meanings as well. For instance, red is passion, blue is calmness, pink is flirtatious, and white is virginity. Even the choice not to wear a wedding gown holds much meaning to the couple. Yet here you sit, calling it just a dress. Shame on you, Sherlock." Flora plopped herself on the sofa and Mrs. Hudson went to her to calm her lest she reinjured herself, as she was still very early in the healing process.

Holmes looked nonplussed. He looked at me, and I shrugged

my shoulders to say this is just you. He went to Flora on bended knee and said, "My darling woman, I had no idea of these meanings. I should have guessed that everything in a wedding has meaning. To be honest, I only said that…." At this point, Holmes' voice lowered and he began to mumble. Flora looked at him quizzically as even she, sitting so closely, did not hear his words.

"Holmes, old man, speak up. We would all like to hear this." I said from my chair.

Holmes turned and glared at me. He cleared his throat and turned back to Flora. "I said I only said what I did to Watson because I was jealous, he was able to see you in your wedding gown and I was not."

Everyone froze on the spot, even Billy, who had come up the stairs with a message, for Holmes, I presume he had been frozen in place. No one moved as time went by. Finally, Billy spoke. "Cor blimey Sherlock. I thought you was above feeling like the rest of us."

We all laughed, even Holmes. Billy entered and said the message was for Holmes, who took it and put it in his pocket. Then he looked at Flora and said, "Are there any more items on your wedding planning list?" Flora pulled the list from her pocket and looked.

"Well, let's see," Flora said. "Mycroft will perform the

ceremony. Doctor Watson will be standing up for you, and Mrs. Hudson will stand up for me. The church, St. Bride's, is booked. Invitations are sent and everyone already replied. There will be 52 at the church. There will just be family and close friends at the reception. The cake will be made by William Rich as his pastry shop is across the street from St. Bride's and convenient to visit when Mrs. Hudson and I went to confirm the church. The reception will be at 221b. I don't think Sherlock or I are ready for crowds yet. We will have boxes of cake and treats for Billy to hand out to the irregulars after the ceremony. Mycroft has loaned us his carriage for me to get to the church and for us both to return to Baker Street. Flowers for the church, Baker Street and for us will be done by the little shop on Gower Street. I love their attention to detail. Sherlock has the rings and has entrusted their care to Doctor Watson. I believe wedding planning is done, but Mrs. Hudson and I have much planning left for Christmas. We are putting together boxes for the women in Whitechapel. The Salvation Army will pass them out. All will have a comb, mirror, soap, candies, a hair pin, and a bottle of toilette."

"My love, please don't overdo it," said Sherlock. I don't want my bride too tired for her wedding day."

"Sherlock, I haven't done half of what you think I have. Billy and Mrs. Hudson have arranged most of it for me." Flora smiled at Holmes and if you didn't know him as I did, you would miss his internal sigh of relief."

Flora sat back on the sofa and Holmes covered her with a coverlet. I was in my chair, and Mrs. Hudson sat next to Flora. Billy sat in his barrel chair and Holmes returned to his chair and took out the message. We all waited expectantly as we all surmised it was from Lestrade. With that, another knock was heard at the front door and Billy ran to answer it. He came up with another message, this one obviously from Mycroft. Holmes looked at us, "which one first?" We chose Mycroft's unanimously.

Holmes opened the envelope and read. We were all a family now and what one knew all the others knew too. No secrets, none of Holmes holding back things. Holmes began reading, "My dear brother mine, you will be happy to know that the Crown has seized all assets of every Lord on the list. They will have titles removed when Parliament is next in session. The Brigadier has been named a security risk to the Commonwealth and, as such, will spend the rest of his life in one of Her Majesty's 'lovelier' prisons overseas. The Crown has also decided to pay all the women who survive a sum of two hundred pounds each. I was sorry to hear of Flora's friend, Rose, passing last weekend. Please pass my love on to her. Respectfully, Mycroft."

Everyone was pleased to hear all this news. Flora had a hanky to her eyes at the mention of Rose, but we were all told to expect it though we didn't want to believe it. Now Holmes was opening the message from Lestrade, and all were sure that this would not be all good news.

Holmes opened the message and began, "Sherlock, to keep you up to date, we obtained convictions on all the men we arrested. Though some escaped hanging if they did not admit to having bedded certain of the women who have passed, then we had to be satisfied with life. Some admitted to certain women during questioning, and they are to be hanged. Lord, or should I say Mr., Frake is to be hung after the doctors say he is well enough to do so. He is in Bethlem Royal Hospital, Bedlam, for a stay of an unknown duration. As for Thomas Ledingford, we still cannot locate him, but we are narrowing down where he can be. He is penniless and desperate by now. Will keep sending updates, Lestrade."

We sat quietly for a moment and finally, Mrs. Hudson said, "tea and biscuits, anyone?" We all agreed that would be a welcome reprieve from thinking about Thomas still being out there somewhere. The constables were still stationed, two in the front, two in the back. I was sure they would not fit in their uniforms after their stint as our guards because Mrs. Hudson fed them several times a day.

Chapter 51
Christmas Eve

During the next few weeks, time seemed to fly. Holmes and I solved a quick case for Lestrade, Mrs. Hudson and Flora were preparing for Christmas and the wedding, Billy was trying to think of the best treats to include in the wedding boxes for the irregulars, and Lestrade and Gregson were searching for Thomas. We would occasionally meet up at 221b during the day, but we were always there for dinner. Along with discussions of how our day went, Flora and Mrs. Hudson regaled us with details of Christmas and wedding updates.

We all helped decorate the flat for the holidays. Flora did not want the flat to have wedding decorations because the holiday was just that, a holiday for all of us. Holmes had never wanted Christmas decorations in the flat before, but this year he decked the halls with the best of them. The flat looked warm and like a real home. The smell of baking was lovely, too and I know I will be delighted to partake of the treats in a few days.

Holmes showed no signs of nervousness as I did before my wedding. If anything, Flora was the nervous one. She was nervous because Thomas was still at large, out there somewhere. He was a threat to her happiness. He had almost destroyed her twice and she was worried that the third time would be fatal. Holmes and I would never let that happen, of course.

On Christmas Eve, all preparations for the wedding were done, and we readied for our goose dinner and the exchange of our gifts. There would be no time tomorrow. The small tree next to the fireplace seemed dwarfed with the presents stacked under it. Flora and Mrs. Hudson were downstairs finishing the meal preparation and Billy and Holmes were transporting the desserts up the stairs and to the sideboard. They said I could not be trusted! Imagine! There was a rum trifle and figgy pudding with a large bowl of brandy butter next to it. There was shortbread and candied fruits. Mrs. Hudson made a bread pudding with custard because she knew Holmes was most fond of it. I remained in my chair so they could not say I was sneaking a taste, but oh, how I wanted to.

Eventually, we all sat with brandied eggnog and had a moment of calm before dinner was ready. Lestrade and Gregson were invited with their wives, but they had not arrived nor sent word. They were hard on the search for Thomas, who had been sighted this afternoon. Just as we were going to toast to their health and luck, they arrived at Baker Street. They relieved the constables to go home to their families. They had caught Thomas. Finally. They came directly here from the Yard where he was safely behind bars. They had both sent their wives to family members for the holiday because they didn't know how long the search would be, so they made themselves comfortable and Flora handed them each an eggnog and kissed their cheeks.

When they had rested a bit, they began to tell us how Thomas had been captured. "you would never believe it," said Lestrade, "it was actually a friend of Billy's who spotted him. Another irregular, Wiggins, I think it was, was visiting family west of London. He spotted him in Chiswick Gardens. There was a gardener's shed he had broken into and was living in. It was over quickly. I think he had had enough. He was cold and wet and looked half-starved. He's in jail now in time for his Christmas dinner."

"Ah, Wiggins," Holmes said. "He's the head of the irregulars on a much-needed break with the little family he still has. He was at Baker Street right after all of this happened. Billy here, his lieutenant, showed him a picture of Ledingford. The thanks goes to Billy as well." We all raised our glasses in a hip-hip hooray for him and Billy blushed to the tips of his ears.

"What will happen now?" asked Flora. It was easy to see she was still nervous and justifiably so.

Gregson said, "He has had his charges read and with no money now for legal representation, he will likely have to wait until some young legal upstart wants to make a name for himself and take his case. We have him in a holding cell, but he will be transferred to Pentonville to be held because of the notoriety of this case. We almost couldn't get in our own doors there today. He will be securely held until trial and then hanged. We are transferring him tomorrow under secure detail. Feel safe, Miss James. Tomorrow you become Mrs. Sherlock Holmes." We all raised our glasses in a toast to Mrs. Sherlock Holmes. Flora was beaming, but not nearly as much as Holmes when he heard Flora called by her soon-to-be married name.

Flora and Mrs. Hudson went to check the dinner. Billy went down to the kitchen to help carry and, of course, get first taste! Holmes, once they left, turned to Lestrade and asked if there were any worries about their notorious prisoner.

"No, Sherlock," Lestrade said, "he came willingly. He looked defeated. But once he warmed up, he yelled throughout the jail about Flora's attributes and how he bedded her first and took the one thing a woman can give her husband. He cursed the unfortunates he had abducted and blamed them for not being more willing and accommodating to his ilk, forcing him into abducting and drugging them into submission. To be honest, he never shuts up. We can't wait to get him to Pentonville. Maybe they can shut him up."

Holmes was angered by this. It would be easy for a constable, a reporter, or anyone hearing Thomas to have something in the paper tomorrow on Flora's day. Lestrade read his mind. 'Sherlock, there are no newspapers tomorrow on Christmas Day to ruin things for Flora." Holmes smiled and thanked him for reminding him of that and for getting Ledingford out before there were newspapers coming out.

With that, our Christmas dinner began to arrive. What wasn't set on the table was lined up alongside the desserts on the sideboard. Goose, and sage and onion stuffing with chestnuts. Roast carrots and potatoes. Brussel sprouts. And mash with gravy. Finally, lots of pigs in a blanket, those lovely little bacon-wrapped sausages. We sat and ate and talked about the wedding, families, love, and the bravery of women.

When coffee and dessert were served, we began opening presents. We all chipped in and got Billy a nice new winter coat and boots. Lestrade and Gregson got him a scarf in the same colour as Scotland Yard constable uniforms. The men, as always, got their favourite cigars, or tobacco, or bottle. We all decided to get Mrs. Hudson a ticket to visit her sister and a lovely new hat to wear on the journey. Flora got Sherlock a new set of leather-bound scrapbooks to paste all the clippings he hadn't room for in the old. Sherlock got Flora a beautiful new dress and hat to wear as they travelled to Brighton on boxing day for their honeymoon. Both were in her favourite colours of, navy and pink. They matched her moonstone engagement ring perfectly. All in all, we had a wonderful Christmas Eve with the happiness we all needed after the long ordeal to stop the horrible sex trafficking ring. And tomorrow, why tomorrow will be the wedding of Sherlock Holmes!

The Keeper of the Flame

Mary, Mary, quite contrary. You shall pay, and pay dearly. I have lost everything. You have made me like this. The sight of you, the thought of you, the smell of you. I am obsessed. If only you gave yourself willingly to me the first time I wanted you all those years ago, I would not be here. Here in this filthy jail. Me. Lord Thomas Blackwell Ledingford. I would have given those whores purpose. A way to serve men. But you and your precious Sherlock took that away from them too. You ruin everything. You must be gone from my life, from this life. Beware my moth, as there are still those who will help me. Did you not think there were men in Scotland Yard who were not in my club? I am coming for you today and thanks to my friends in the Yard, I know where, when, and how. I'm coming for you, Mary. I'm coming... I'm coming... I'm coming...

Chapter 52

The Wedding with an Interlude

The day dawned glorious and unseasonably warm. Christmas day. The wedding day. As I came downstairs, Holmes and Flora were awake along with Mrs. Hudson and Billy having a light breakfast of coddled eggs and toast and tea. I sat for my share. Holmes and Billy and I will be going to the church to get ready. Our wedding clothes were awaiting us there. We enjoyed a leisurely and quiet breakfast. Just the four of us. It would be a busy day.

As Mrs. Hudson was to be with us and the reception was to be here, we would need someone to be here and tidy the flat and await the caterer's, which was Mycroft's present to the bride and groom, but really to Mrs. Hudson but she never would accept it, so it was given to the couple. Mrs. Hudson had her friend from her church, Miss Dawn Parks, come to do the light cleaning and to help the caterers set up the food while she was at the wedding. Billy escorted her up the stairs just now and took her coat and offered her tea and toast. I could see why Billy was being a little gentleman. Miss Parks was very pretty. I could also see I would need to escort Mrs. Hudson to her weekly church services quite soon.

Miss Parks took right over, cleaning the remnants of breakfast away so we could finish our tea and say our goodbyes. I told Billy to call a growler, not a hansom, and have it wait. He knew what to do. Then I checked my room to make sure I had everything. The rings were safely inside my coat pocket. I told Billy to check his room to ensure he had everything and to come back upstairs.

Flora and Holmes were standing by the front bay window, holding each other tenderly. The last single moments for soon they would be husband and wife. Mrs. Hudson and I stood watching the couple and, I assumed we were both thinking of what they had suffered to get here. It turns out Holmes and Flora had been watching each other for months. Doing a little dance of he or she would never like me until that fateful day of the knife. Love it was and love it will always be until death do us part. They were good for each other, both with that logical way of thought. Holmes had taught himself that at an early age, though he was probably predisposed to that way of thought from birth. Flora was probably predisposed too, but she had been teaching herself only for the last few years. She had made quite the long strides and was developing her brain nicely. Holmes, I knew, was quite proud of her. I tapped Mrs. Hudson's arm, and we made our way downstairs to see if she needed help, though if truth be told, I was going to see if Miss Dawn Parks needed help!

Chapter Interlude

I stood holding Flora in my arms. I never wanted to let her go. When you live your life believing one thing and you find out something else, totally different, was true, it's shocking to the mind. Watson was right. I never understood love. Not until now. This person, so like me, so intelligent, but so understanding and gentle and kind and brave, loved me. Once that happened, I, too, understood love. Now she is to be my wife. She is to solve crimes too, using my methods yet understanding them better than I do. I am a lucky man, indeed.

I stood in Sherlock's arms, thinking about how I got here. I had loved him for months. I stalked him like a schoolgirl, knowing he knew I was. I didn't care. Just the sight of him made me weak. Then, that night when I awoke in his bed with his kiss on my forehead, I knew he loved me too. This last case took my ability to bear him a child away, but he told me we already had children, the irregulars, and we could adopt because there were so many unwanted children on the streets of London and its filled orphanages. My Sherlock has more heart and more understanding than he admits to, and more than he realizes. Here, now, I know in a few short hours, I will be his wife, his partner in life. And I, too, shall solve crimes, albeit of a different nature, but he is nonetheless proud of me for it. I am a lucky woman indeed.

Back to our chapter...

All of us were packing up forgotten things and asking did you remember this or that, and poor Miss Parks was trying to work around us and trying to shove us all out the door to give her some peace to clean. Maybe she would stay at the reception if I asked her nicely? Finally, we trundled into the growler and off to the church we went bearing the forgotten bits with us and leaving the women in peace.

Once the growler left, Mrs. Hudson went and poured us a brandy, medicinal, of course. Even Miss Parks was glad to have one at this point. We stood quietly for a moment, and Miss Parks left to ready the kitchen for the food. Mrs. Hudson went down with her to bring up my gown. We couldn't trust Sherlock with it up here, for surely, he would peek. I went into our bedroom and readied my toilette. I was wearing little makeup, just some rouge and lipstick, and I glossed my lashes a bit. I was never a redhead, as the papers reported after my 'death.' The real Flora James was. I have dark hair, wavy, with pale skin and dark lashes and a rosebud-hued mouth. My mam called me Rosebud when I was a babe.

Mrs. Hudson brought the gown in and hung it behind the door. My undergarments and chemise were on the bed, and we began. As I was being helped to dress, Mrs. Hudson spoke, "Flora, we have been through a lot in the recent weeks. I want you to know you have become like a daughter to me as much as Sherlock has become like a son over the years we have known each other. I love you very much and I'm so glad you will be living here with us in this little family of strange people." She began to cry, and I held her.

"Mrs. Hudson, I love you too. You are a brave woman. I'm glad to be here too. We are a strange little family indeed, but there is so much love in this family. So much trust and understanding within our family too. We respect each other. That makes us work well together. Now let's get back on track and get dressed. I don't want to be late for my own wedding!

We both finished dressing and came out of the bedroom to a beautiful scene. We had heard the catering people arrive, so we knew they were there, but we did not expect what we saw. The wedding cake sat in the centre of the table in a circle of billowing tulle and lace. It was from out of a fairy tale dream. The room had been draped with the same tulle and lace and flowers were set into every section of it. The bay windows were swathed in the tulle and lace with flowers set on the sill. The sideboard was set with the silver awaiting the food and champagne flutes and a champagne bucket sat awaiting the fizz. Added to the Christmas decorations, it was beautiful. It was like a dream. Miss Parks was there with a hanky to her eyes. Mrs. Hudson and I cried when we saw it too. I went back to the bedroom to touch up my face. When I came out of the bedroom once again, Billy was there to escort Mrs. Hudson and me to the church. His eyes were wide in looking at me in my gown. We said our goodbyes to Miss Parks and went down the stairs, where the driver and Billy handed us into the coach. A crowd had gathered wishing me well and Billy and the driver took their places, and we were off to St. Bride's. I was getting married!

The Wedding

Holmes was pacing in the back of the church. He looked out for the hundredth time at the array of flowers lining the steps to the church. "Old man, your staring holes through the church entrance will not make her get here faster."

Mycroft was with us and said, "Come, brother, mine. We belong at the altar. My men stationed along the way said she will be arriving shortly." He patted Sherlock's shoulder and Sherlock turned toward the front of the church.

I stepped in behind them and I heard Sherlock say, "Mycroft, I want to thank you for all you have done for Flora and me. I want you to know how much I appreciate it." Mycroft whispered, "I do, little brother, I do."

We took our places; the guests were already seated. Lestrade and Gregson were sat in front with their wives, both of whom had their hankies at the ready. The church was filled with irregulars, and they had even tried to wash up. Several constables were there. The booksmith and his wife were there with their daughter. She was still quite frail from her ordeal. Love was in this building as we heard the coach arrive. The music from the organist began and Mrs. Hudson began her walk up the main aisle. She was smiling and teary and the guests stood and smiled back at her.

Then Flora entered the church. The sunlight beaming behind her. I saw Holmes stagger on his feet and both Mycroft and I reached out to hold him up. Flora then walked the aisle and there wasn't a whisper. Just the music, her, and her groom in tears as he watched her.

She arrived at the altar and Holmes held her hand. Mycroft began the ceremony. He was as somber as a minister, but he beamed at the couple. We all did. We waited for the best parts.

"Do you, Sherlock Holmes, take Flora James to be your wife, to have and to hold from this day forward, for better, for worse, for richer, for poorer, in sickness and in health, to love and to cherish, till death do you part, according to God's holy law?

"I do,"

"Do you, Flora James, take Sherlock Holmes to be your husband, to have and to hold from this day forward, for better, for worse, for richer, for poorer, in sickness and in health, to love and to cherish, till death do you part, according to God's holy law?"

"I do."

"By the power vested in me by the Church of England and by The Crown, I now pronounce you husband and wife, Sherlock, kiss your wife!"

Holmes gladly obliged and kissed his new wife with gusto, even bending her backward to the delight of everyone in the church.

Everyone stood and congratulated the couple as they walked down the aisle of the church.

They exited to walk down the steps and into the coach. As the couple proceeded to cheers from those inside the church and those who had gathered outside to wish them well, the driver of the coach stood and was waving his hands and shouting and pointing. Holmes looked at him quizzically and followed with his eyes the direction the driver was pointing. Then time seemed to stop. Holmes grabbed Flora and held her close to him so his back was facing the direction the driver was pointing to and a shot rang out.

I looked to the direction of the shot and saw two armed constables shoot Thomas Ledingford. I looked back to Holmes, but he wasn't there. I looked to the bottom of the steps and saw Holmes still holding Flora. The shot had gone through Holmes and exited Flora, shooting them both with one bullet. Time seemed to speed up again and people were screaming. Lestrade and Gregson ran to the now-dead Thomas and the constables who stood over him. I ran to Holmes and Flora, pushing people out of my way.

Husband and wife…

The crimson blood ran out of them, mingling on Flora's gown in wild abstract patterns and on the ground underneath them. They were facing, still in each other's arms. Sherlock was looking at Flora as her eyes softly closed. He whispered, "I love you, Mrs. Holmes," as his eyes gently closed too.

THE END

In my novel, there is mention of trafficking children. Unfortunates, and poorer women were trafficked, but it was also quite common to traffic children. When Lord Ledingford says he wasn't so bad now, he meant even he would not stop this low. There is a short article by Caroline Warfield on that topic. I've also included a list of further resources.

Selected Resources on child sex trafficking and the sex trafficking of Women in Victorian London

Child Trafficking in the Nineteenth Century by Caroline Warfield from Dirty, Sexy History

Cossins, Anne. Masculinities, Sexualities, and Child Sexual Abuse. Martinus Nijhoff Publishers, Feb 16, 2000, pp. 6-7.

"Custody of Infants," Commons and Lords Hansard, the Official Report of Debates in Parliament, HL Deb 18 July 1839 vol 49 cc485-94.

"Custody Rights and Domestic Violence," UK Parliament: Living Heritage.

Pietsch, Roland. "Ships Boys and Youth Culture in Eighteenth-Century Britain," The Northern Mariner: Online Edition, Canadian Nautical Research Society.

Venning, Annabel. "Britain's Child Slaves," The Daily Mail, 17 September 2010.

https://www.google.com/url?sa=t&source=web&rct=j&url=
https://www.repository.law.indiana.edu/cgi/viewcontent.cgi%3Fart
icle%3D1045%26context%3Dijlse&ved=2ahUKEwi2o6jrwfz8Ah
UmFFkFHSWjAfMQFnoECDoQAQ&usg=AOvVaw3Jp-
oVyM2v5vx8oQ mouyih

https://www.google.com/url?sa=t&source=web&rct=j&url=https://
www.repository.law.indiana.edu/cgi/viewcontent.cgi%3Farticle%3
D1045%26context%3Dijlse&ved=2ahUKEwi2o6jrwfz8AhUmFFk
FHSWjAfMQFnoECDoQAQ&usg=AOvVaw3Jp-
oVyM2v5vx8oQ mouyih

The following is an excellent source I have used in scholarly research as a professor.

https://www.brandeis.edu/projects/fse/slavery/contemporary/essay-
historical-discourses.html

To see what happens to Sherlock and his new bride, look for the next book, Brighton Rock on the Beach, coming in the fall/winter of 2023.

You can follow my Facebook page F.D. Hunt for updates as well. Be on the lookout for my upcoming Sherlock Holmes cookbook too!!!

About the Author

Florence Diana Hunt was born in Valhalla, NY. She lived between NYC and Lee-on-the-Solent in the UK for a good part of her childhood. When she was an adjunct professor she lived between upstate NY and London. She has two doctorates and several certifications. Under the Pale Yellow Street Lamp is her first novel. She has also written a memoir, a short story about her daughter Amy's death from Reye's Syndrome, and a fairy tale with ex Trans Siberian Orchestra singer, the late Maxx Mann. She is currently writing book two in the Trilogy of Sherlock Holmes and Flora James, Brighton Rock on the Beach. There is also a tie in cookbook in the works with recipes from the foods mentioned in both the Arthur Conan Doyle canon and her trilogy.

Florence lives in upstate NY but visits England as often as possible as it is her true home. Writing is her passion and we will be seeing more great work from her. She lives with her husband and two dogs, Birdie and Butterscotch. Her two boys are grown, one is a gifted guitarist, one with a family of his own with his high school sweetheart and true love. Florence also worked in the mental health field handling crisis calls on a warm line after retiring from teaching. She now is fully retired and writes full time. Another passion of hers is cooking. She has a truly impressive cookbook collection and will one day add her cookbook to it.

When Florence moves on from Sherlock and Flora, she will be writing another fairy tale she collaborated on with Maxx Mann before his untimely death. She also has a paranormal novel set in the UK in the works as well as a love story based on her life.

www.ingramcontent.com/pod-product-compliance
Lightning Source LLC
Chambersburg PA
CBHW071322120626
46546CB00002B/399